W9-ATF-772

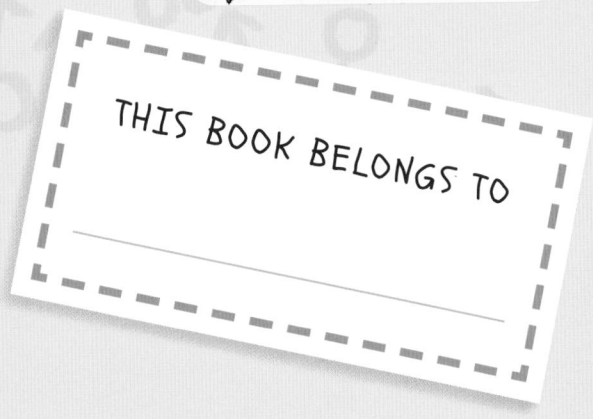
THIS BOOK BELONGS TO

_____

The
Middle
School
Rules of

BRIAN URLACHER

as told by
Sean Jensen

BroadStreet
PUBLISHING

BroadStreet Publishing Group LLC
Racine, Wisconsin, USA
www.broadstreetpublishing.com

The Middle School Rules of Brian Urlacher

ISBN 978-1-4245-4979-5 (hard cover)
ISBN 978-1-4245-5010-4 (e-book)

Brian Urlacher is represented by Bryce Karger and Brenda Lundberg–Casey of Image Athlete Marketing.

Photograph of Brian Urlacher provided by The Chicago Bears. All rights reserved.

Illustrated by Max Smith
Cover and interior design by Garborg Design Works | garborgdesign.com
Editorial services provided by Ginger Garrett | gingergarrett.com
    and Michelle Winger | literallyprecise.com

Printed in China

15 16 17 18 19 20 21   7 6 5 4 3 2 1

FOREWORD

It was the 1992 football season, and I was in my second season as the head coach at Lovington High School. I decided to go to a junior high game on a Thursday. I don't remember the opponent, but I do remember a scraggly freshman catching a long touchdown pass.

It wasn't that spectacular of a catch, probably like ones you've seen caught by typical 15-year-olds. This kid was like a hundred other young football players I had seen. I had heard he was a little taller and faster than average, but nothing really outstanding. Heck, I could barely pronounce his last name!

Brian URLACHER.

I didn't know how this young man would impact my life. He went from a scrawny ninth grader to the ninth overall pick in the NFL Draft in 2000—making spectacular plays along the way.

I've been asked a lot, "When did you know Urlacher was going to be an NFL star?"

I didn't.

But Brian had the characteristics it takes to succeed at the highest levels—characteristics you'll read about in this book. Brian developed physically, but his personal qualities are what also drove him to be a future Hall of Famer. He had work ethic, commitment, dedication, perseverance, and humility.

You can develop these same characteristics. A circle of support can help guide you, but ultimately it is up to you. Every young person who reads this book possesses the qualities Brian had. With a little help, you can achieve more than you think is possible.

I have often said the football field is a modern day "rites of passage," where boys become men. I'm proud to have been a small part of that development in Brian. I admire the incredible man he has become—on and off the field. His love for his family is unsurpassed. His dedication to his children is unequivocal. His generosity to his friends and community is undeniable. His commitment to his teammates is unwavering.

Brian came from good stock. His mother, Lavoyda, was a special parent. She sacrificed to make sure Sheri, Brian, and Casey were taken care of. I liken Brian to one of my favorite quotes by Frank Lloyd Wright, "No stream rises higher than its source."

Brian rose high—a tribute to a mother's love and sacrifice.

Enjoy the book. Learn about Brian, his friends, and his family. But mostly, learn about yourself.

Coach Speedy Faith
Lovington High School

Dear Reader,

Thanks for picking up my story.

Looking back, I didn't spend much time thinking about what I didn't have, or what I couldn't do.

I learned that from my mother.

She often said two things: "Get it done," and "Don't make excuses."

That's how I live and that's how I want my kids to live.

Whatever your circumstances, I hope you focus on the positives in your life and not the negatives.

Best wishes,

Table of Contents

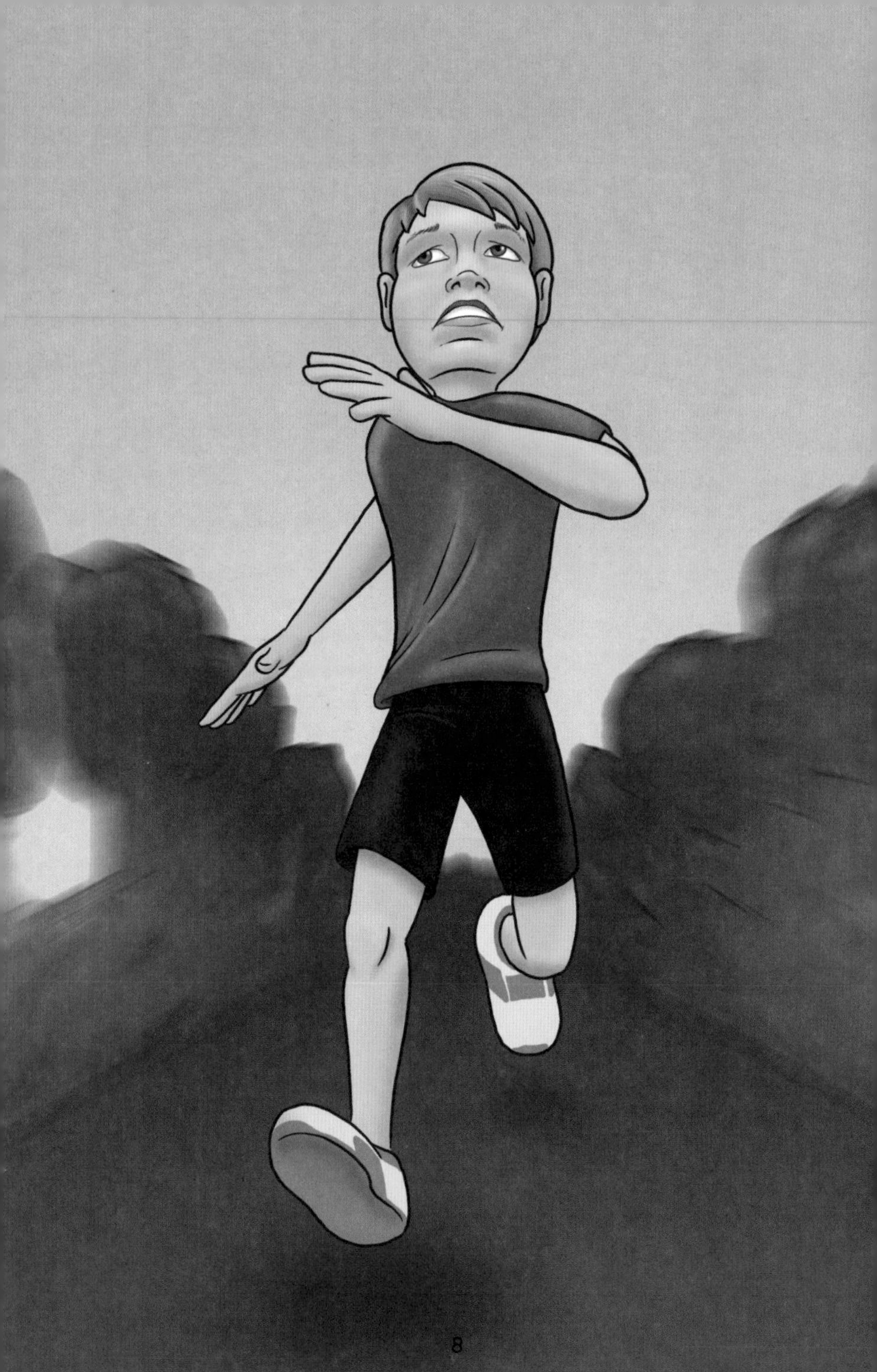

Chapter 1

Finding His Way

In sixth grade, Brian Urlacher was shy and small, just a kid trying to fit in at Taylor Middle School in Lovington, New Mexico. Brian tried to stay out of trouble...until trouble found him.

Charles was one of his best buddies in elementary school, but he was annoyed at Brian. Brian couldn't figure out why, but that didn't matter in sixth grade.

So once the final school bell rang at 3:10 p.m., Brian bolted for home—with Charles in hot pursuit. Brian didn't like confrontation, let alone with Charles who was bigger *and* had facial hair!

I don't know how to fight, Brian thought. *I just want to get home.*

He zigzagged through the neighborhood—sticking close to 11th Street—toward his house on Avenue M about ten blocks south of the school. When Brian got home, panting and sweating, he slammed the front door shut and made a beeline for his bedroom.

After four or five days, Charles stopped chasing Brian home. Charles never told Brian why he was mad, but Brian realized middle school rules don't always make sense.

Later in the school year, Brian knew exactly what set another kid off.

Brian and Ty were on the same basketball team, and Brian thought Ty was being a ball hog.

"Pass the ball! Pass the ball!" his teammates shouted.

They got smoked in a game to 21.

After the loss, Brian complained, "Maybe if someone wasn't playing one on five, we could have actually made it a game."

Ty, who had a reputation for being tough, didn't want to hear it. In the locker room, he climbed on top of Brian and punched him on the side of his head. Brian didn't want to fight, but he also didn't want to get hurt. He didn't know any karate and he didn't know how to box, so he did what came naturally: Brian pushed Ty off and then tackled him.

The force of Brian's tackle knocked the wind out of Ty, who fell hard to the locker room floor. Just then, Mr. Dobbs entered and separated the boys. He sent both Ty and Brian to detention!

"But he started it!" Brian protested.

Didn't matter.

Brian had always stayed out of trouble, and he didn't know how his mother would react. But at dinnertime when they talked about the scuffle, she wasn't mad at him.

"I don't want you kids starting fights," Brian's mother said, "but sometimes you have to end them."

The best part of sixth grade for Brian was finding his best friend, Brandon. The relationship was forged during lunchtime. After they ate, along with other boys, Brian and Brandon would play basketball or football, often against each other.

Basketball was their favorite sport. And while Brian was good, Brandon was great.

Even before Brian knew him, he recalled Brandon starring in Little Dribblers, the local rec program. Brandon was quick, he could shoot threes...and he could dribble the ball with both hands! Plus, his uncle was Chief Bridgforth, the head coach of the high school varsity team.

Brandon had it made.

Being cooped up in a

house playing video games and watching TV wasn't their thing. Brian and Brandon liked to ride their bikes all over town, exploring, looking for games, or having a home run derby in the street.

But their absolute favorite thing was playing basketball at Ben Alexander Elementary School—just a long football toss from Lovington High School.

They really liked the eight-foot-high rims.

Brian, Brandon, and other boys from the neighborhood would play full-court games, pretending to be "Like Mike," flying through the air for majestic dunks like the Chicago Bulls superstar.

There were so many players at Ben Alexander that a team was always waiting to play the winner.

Pretty much everyone could dunk, so they'd often get cuts on their fingers.

"Look at mine," someone would boast afterwards.

"Ewwww!" everyone else would yell.

The boys would all wear bandages to school, but they always returned the next day.

The games sometimes got rough, usually between Brian and his little brother Casey, but there was one rule: Don't break or bend the rims. That wasn't a problem for the regulars; it was the visitors who would go too far and dunk with too much force.

The boys didn't know who maintained the court which was

next to a playground; they just knew someone regularly replaced the nets.

But a broken or bent rim? That could take weeks to fix. They learned this the hard way, when Jimmy's cousin from Lubbock got too excited. He went up in the air like he was Charles Barkley, slamming the ball through the hoop...and tearing it all up.

But who was going to say something to Jimmy's cousin? He was bigger than everyone. None of the boys had the nerve to yell at him, so they nervously laughed—and they all went home early that day.

The imaginary season continued weeks later.

Brian was the star of the Mavericks, Brandon the star of the Rockets. And because Brian didn't like to play *with* his little brother Casey, he often played *against* him. Casey was a good player, and one of them would get too rough defending the other, then they'd start pushing and shoving until Brandon broke it up.

"Come on, guys! Do we have to do this every time?"

They'd play hoops for hours and hours, and when the streetlights turned on, they'd hop on their bikes and ride home.

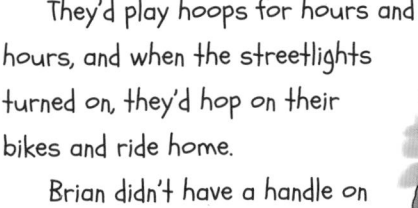

Brian didn't have a handle on middle school yet. But he was thankful that Lovington was safe enough for him to play until dark.

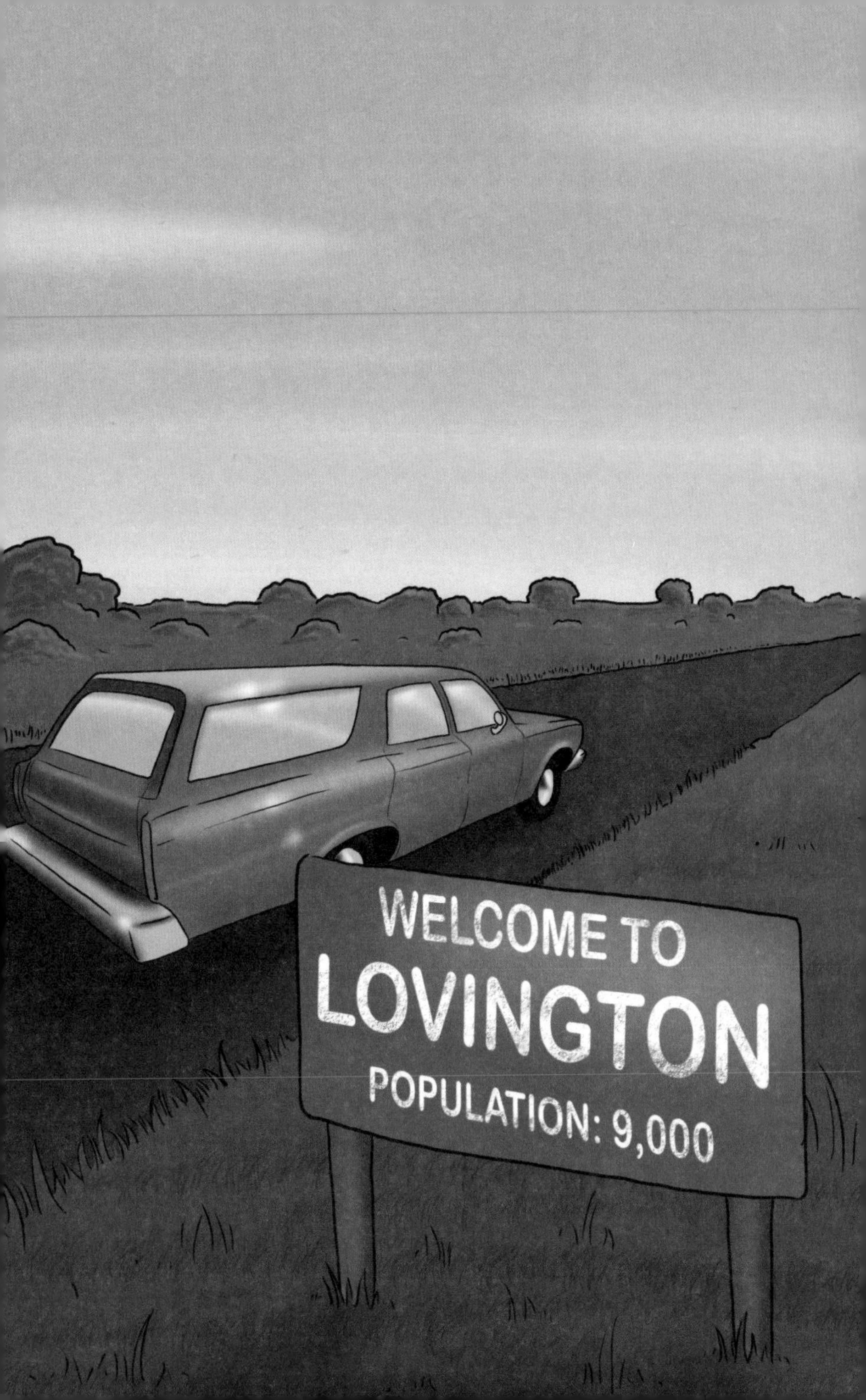
WELCOME TO
LOVINGTON
POPULATION: 9,000

Chapter 2

Lovington

Brian was born on May 25, 1978, in Pasco, Washington. Brian's mother, Lavoyda, married Brad Urlacher when she was very young, and they had Sheri, Brian, and Casey, in that order. About a year separated Sheri from Brian and Brian from Casey.

Brian was seven when his parents divorced in the winter of 1985, and he and his brother and sister moved to Lovington, in southeastern New Mexico. He was sad and nervous, but it helped

that his mom's parents lived in a nearby town.

Lovington was named after the first storefront there, the Jim B. Love Grocery Store, which was built in 1908. Most parents worked in farming, ranching, or oil drilling.

Lovington had about nine thousand people and was mostly middle-class, which meant not too many people drove fancy cars— especially the cars from Germany or Italy. It was the sort of town where everyone knew everyone, so the high school kids didn't bother trying to get into R-rated movies because someone at the theater would know their actual age.

Brian's grandparents weren't very far away, but he noticed his mother didn't ask for their help much. Brian's mother worked at least two jobs, neither of them high paying or glamorous, to support her family. Brian's family bounced around at first, sometimes living in trailers or apartments, moving when Lavoyda could find a cheaper place to rent.

Back-to-school shopping was easy.

They'd head to Walmart or Kmart in neighboring towns, where Brian, Casey, and Sheri each got to pick out one pair of shoes, two pair of pants, and a couple of shirts. They couldn't afford to shop at the department store Bealls on Avenue D, near the tall white water tower that read, "Lovington Wildcats."

Bealls had brand names; they had to pick no names.

The boys didn't know it, but their Aunt Dena would take Sheri on a separate shopping trip and get her some extra clothes and shoes.

Not that they ever noticed.

Brian and Casey didn't care about clothes. They cared about sports and bike rides and made-up games. They invented Buck 'Em Bronco, using a 55-gallon plastic drum and stringing four ropes to it attached with used car springs. One boy would climb on the plastic drum while the other frantically tried to knock him off.

It's a wonder neither ever got hurt, but they'd do it until their arms were too exhausted to pull the ropes anymore.

Despite working constantly, Lavoyda always showed up for Sheri's basketball and softball games, and whatever sport Brian and Casey were into. Sometimes, you could hear her before you could see her.

"GO (fill in child's name)!" "COME ON (fill in team's name)!"

"Why does she have to be so loud?" Casey asked Brian.

"Who knows," Brian replied.

But all three kids appreciated that she was there, encouraging them after good plays or bad plays and making her presence known. She quickly learned the names of all their teammates, shouting encouragement to whoever was at the plate or on the free throw line.

Other parents loved Lavoyda because of her outgoing personality and her positivity. She was a people person.

But her favorite people were babies.

If they went to the grocery store, and she saw one, she'd

immediately reach out and say to the parent, "Give me that baby!"

"Mom, you're so embarrassing," Sheri would say.

Lavoyda knew everyone, and everyone knew her. She had two rules: "Get it done," and "Finish what you start."

She wasn't big on excuses, which the kids recognized by her daily commitment to punching the clock wherever she was working, whether it was the Clean Machine or the Town and Country convenience store.

In fourth grade, Brian wanted to quit baseball. If he struck out, Brian would cry. If he didn't get on base, Brian would cry. That season, playing for the Comets, Brian cried a lot—and he was tired of it.

"I stink at baseball. I quit!" Brian told his mother after a game in the middle of the season.

"Oh no you're not," Lavoyda told him in the special, serious voice she didn't use that often. "You can choose not to play next year, but you're going to finish this season, no matter how bad it gets."

"Come on, Mom," Brian protested.

But, like usual, he obeyed his mother.

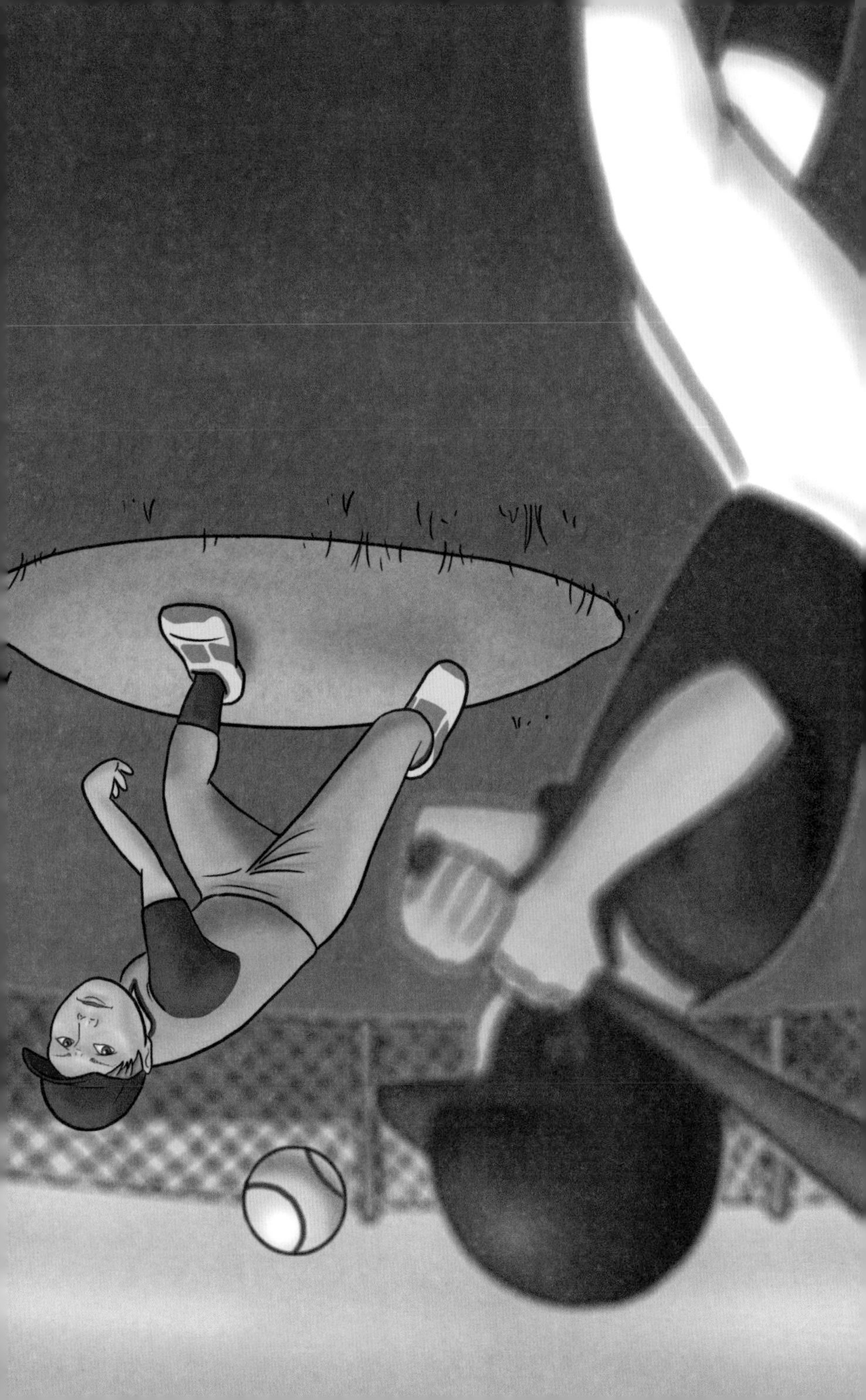

Chapter 3

Sibling Rivalry

Casey was a pest—at least from Brian's point of view. He was 15 months younger, and he was always around.

Since they moved a few times, Casey was a good companion. He liked many of the same things as Brian. Put them in a competitive situation, though, and they were bound to fight—like when they played basketball at Ben Alexander Elementary School.

When Brian was in the seventh grade, both boys signed up to play baseball. In Lovington's "Major League," brothers were usually placed on the same team to make life a little easier for a parent shuttling them to and from practice.

At tryouts, Casey distinguished himself as a hitter, Brian as a pitcher.

But when the coaches gathered to draft their players, Casey had a request: He didn't want to be part of a package deal with his big brother.

"I don't want to play with him," Casey told his mother.

Casey ended up on the Mariners, and Brian on the Braves.

Their teams excelled, although everyone in the family circled one date in particular: June 9, 1990. On that Saturday, the Braves would play the Mariners and—as fate would have it—Brian would pitch.

Casey was the cleanup hitter for the Mariners, and he had a man on second, with two outs in the first inning. Brian reared back and chucked a fastball toward the plate.

"Ball one!"

The first pitch was low and outside.

Brian's second pitch didn't find the strike zone. Casey didn't even swing.

"Ball two!"

Brian was getting a bit nervous now.

So on his third pitch, with all might, Brian flung his fastest fastball toward the plate—and Casey launched it into left center field. The ball landed short of the fence but bounced over it for a ground-rule double.

The Mariners took a 1-0 lead, and Brian was upset on the mound.

Brian hit a harmless dribbler to second base in his first at-bat, and the Braves were still losing 1-0 when Casey got up to the plate again.

With his first pitch, Brian flung his fastest fastball toward the plate—and drilled Casey on the left side of his body. Brian wasn't alarmed. He just glared at his little brother, who hadn't been able to move out of the way of the pitch quickly enough.

Casey didn't say anything. He didn't charge the mound. He just strolled to first base.

That made Brian even angrier.

The Mariners won 3-2.

After the game, Brian's mom asked him what happened on the pitch.

"I hit him in the back...and I don't feel bad about it," Brian said.

Brian's mom could barely keep from laughing since Casey wasn't hurt.

But Casey couldn't resist chiming in, "It's OK, Mom; we won, and I had a great game."

When they got home, Brian was immediately sent to his room, with no snack and no TV time.

Usually, from their bunk beds in the bedroom they always shared, Brian and Casey would talk for a few minutes after Mom tucked them in for the night. But the night after the big game, both worked extra hard *not* to say a word.

Brian fumed and Casey gloated.

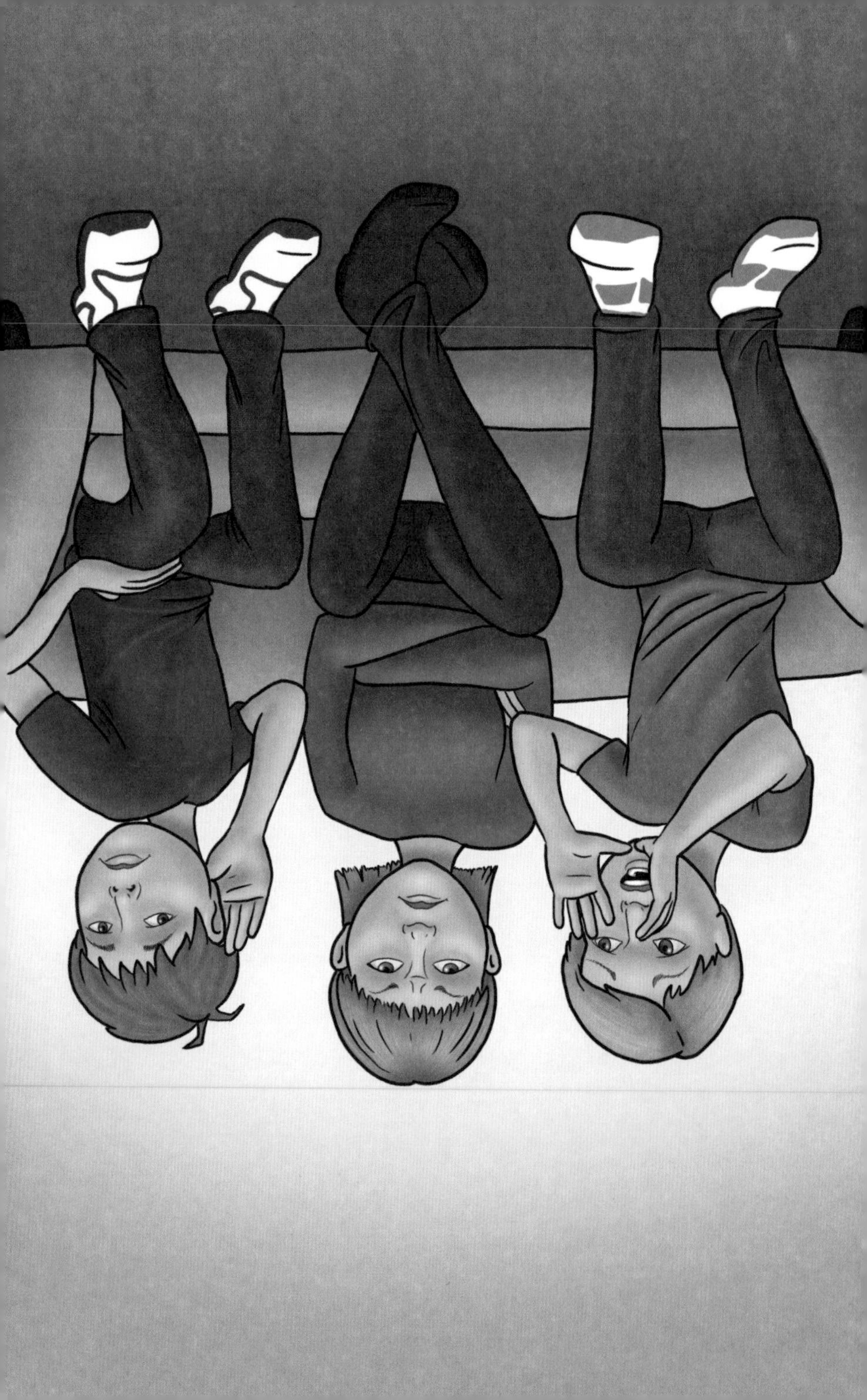

Chapter 4

Ruling the Roost

Brian and Casey clashed often. The only thing they saw eye-to-eye on was their sister Sheri. She was a year older than Brian, and she was bigger and meaner than both of them combined.

Especially when they were in elementary and middle school. Everything the boys did bothered Sheri.

They tried hard to annoy her every chance they could. If she was watching a show, they'd beg her to turn on sports. If she was reading a book, they'd talk really loud.

"HEY CASEY, WHAT ARE WE HAVING FOR DINNER?"

"I DON'T KNOW, BRIAN. MAYBE WE SHOULD ASK SHERI?"

Then they'd both say, "Sheri? Sheri? Sheri? Sheri? Sher..."

Sheri would snap.

"LEAVE ME ALONE!"

She'd storm off to her room, which was definitely off-limits to Brian and Casey.

The family usually lived in apartments or houses that only had one bathroom. Brian and Casey had a favorite gag.

If Sheri was showering, Casey would bang on the locked bathroom door.

"Sheri, I have to go to the bathroom! I can't hold it! Puh-leeze!"

"No, you're going to do something to me," Sheri replied.

"Let me in," Casey begged. "I promise I'm not going to do anything. I gotta go. I gotta go!"

After pretending to go pee, Casey would leave the bathroom—and "forget" to lock the door. Brian would enter with a pitcher of ice water, and dump it over the shower curtain. Then he would run out of the bathroom, and he and Casey would race into their bedroom and lock the door. They would giggle as Sheri screamed at them.

"I'm never going to trust you again!"

Hours or even a day might pass. But eventually, Sheri would retaliate, punching each of them.

And she packed a punch.

To Brian and Casey, it was totally worth it. They loved to bother Sheri.

Sometimes, if she didn't lock her door at night, and she fell asleep first, they would put toothpaste in her hair.

No act, though, went unpunished.

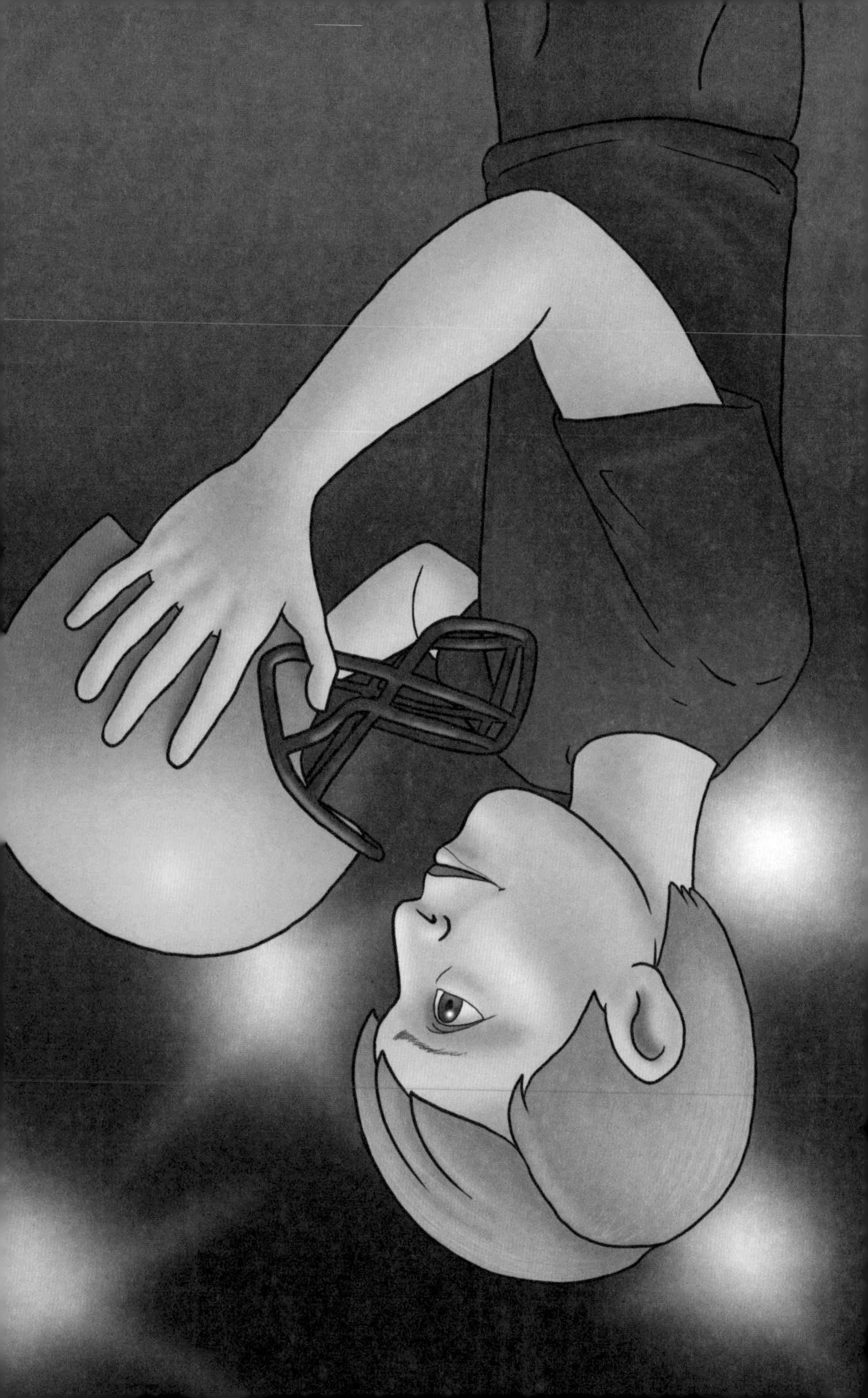

Chapter 5

Football Debut

In Lovington, the boys started playing intramural football in sixth grade. Then they played in pads in seventh grade.

Since Lovington was small, there were only enough players for three teams.

Brian didn't care.

After his first game, Brian ran toward his mom.

"Did you see me score a touchdown? Did you see it?"

"Yes, Brian. Of course I saw it. I'm so proud of you!"

Only moms, dads, and distracted little brothers and sisters were at the games, but Brian still loved to hear the referee blow the whistle after he scored a touchdown.

He instantly fell in love with the game.

Although he wasn't big, Brian liked the contact and the chance to exert all his energy. Plus, he and Brandon played on the same team: the Mustangs! Brandon was the quarterback, and Brian was the fullback.

FOOTBALL DEBUT

The teams didn't throw much, so Brian basically got in the way of a defender and Brandon scrambled through the opening behind his best friend. They were good teammates.

None of the adults kept score or tracked yardage and touchdowns. The games were high scoring, and the boys couldn't keep up with all the points, especially the ones by the other team.

But afterwards, Brian and Brandon would recount how many touchdowns they each scored and how they scored them.

By their unofficial count, Brandon led the Mustangs with 27 touchdowns in six games. Brian had the second-most touchdowns with 19, but he led the team with three interceptions.

Brian enjoyed scoring touchdowns. But he really liked intercepting the ball and trying to return it for a touchdown. He didn't get any defensive touchdowns in his first season, but he sure came close. In one game, he collected a tipped pass for an interception and returned it nearly 30 yards! He got all the way to the other team's five-yard line.

On the very next play, with Brian paving the way, Brandon scored the touchdown.

No one really paid attention to seventh-grade football though. Eighth grade was when it started to matter in Lovington. This was a middle school rule.

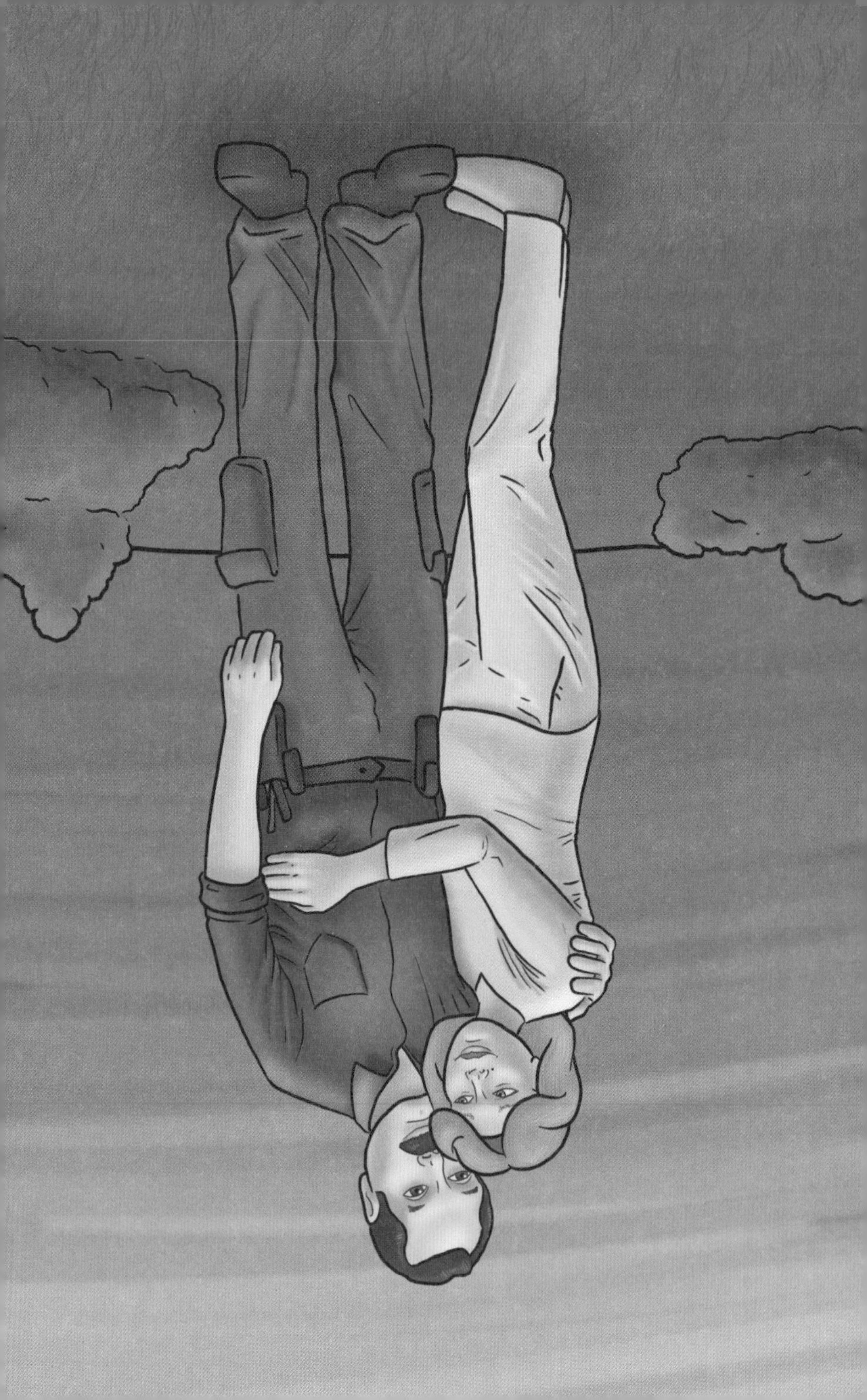

Chapter 6

Father Figure

Another big thing happened in seventh grade: Brian's mom married Troy Leonard. Brian's mom was outgoing and energetic. Troy was the opposite; he didn't say much. Maybe that's why they liked each other, the kids figured.

Things got better when Troy moved in. Mom didn't have to work two jobs because Troy was a pumper. He worked in the oil fields, checking the tanks and deciding when they needed to be emptied. He came home really dirty.

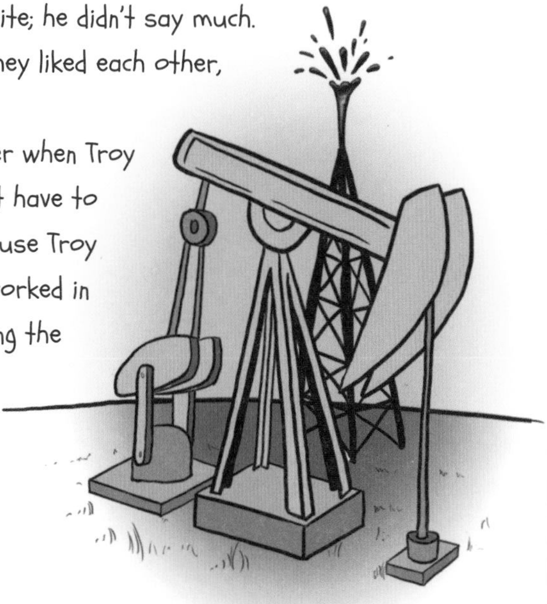

Troy got up very early in the morning—at 4:30 a.m. That meant he went to bed early, so no one was allowed to disturb him with late phone calls. He wanted to be in bed by 9 p.m. No one was supposed to call the house after that time.

If the phone did ring, Brian and Casey would say to each other, "Oh, I hope it's not for me."

Even if the phone rang at 8:30, the boys would hope it wasn't for them.

Brian remembered the first time Brandon called him after 9 p.m. It was 9:05, and Brandon couldn't remember if he had left his football at Brian's house. (He did.)

Troy barked out a comment loud enough so Brandon could hear it too.

"Brian, get off the phone! Does Brandon know you're not to receive a call after nine?"

For every minute you were on, he'd yell something else out. Basically, he would embarrass you. But neither Brian nor Casey got many phone calls, even before bedtime. Nine times out of ten, the calls after 9 p.m. were for Sheri.

"Sheri, get off the phone!"

Sheri didn't always get off right away. A few minutes would pass.

"Sheri, get off the phone!"

Then Sheri would snap, yelling something back. That would get Sheri grounded.

For the boys, there was an even harsher form of punishment than not being able to have fun on the weekend.

Its name was Uncle Henry.

Uncle Henry was a two-foot board with a green handle on one end and two quarter-sized air holes on the opposite end. Those holes allowed Uncle Henry to zip through the air even faster.

Uncle Henry resided next to Troy's bedside and was used to dole out punishment for serious offenses. If you lied or cheated, you'd get swatted by Uncle Henry. If you got into trouble at school, you'd get swatted by Uncle Henry.

Brian, Casey, and Sheri didn't deal with Uncle Henry much. Troy was strict, but he also liked to have fun. He would wrestle with the boys, pretending he was Andre the Giant and they were a tag-team trying to take him down.

Troy also liked to pull pranks on them.

If they started nodding off in his truck, he'd slam on the brakes and scream, "Ahhhhhh!" If it was dark out, he'd jump out from behind a tree and yell.

And the boys learned to approach closed—and partially closed—doors very carefully.

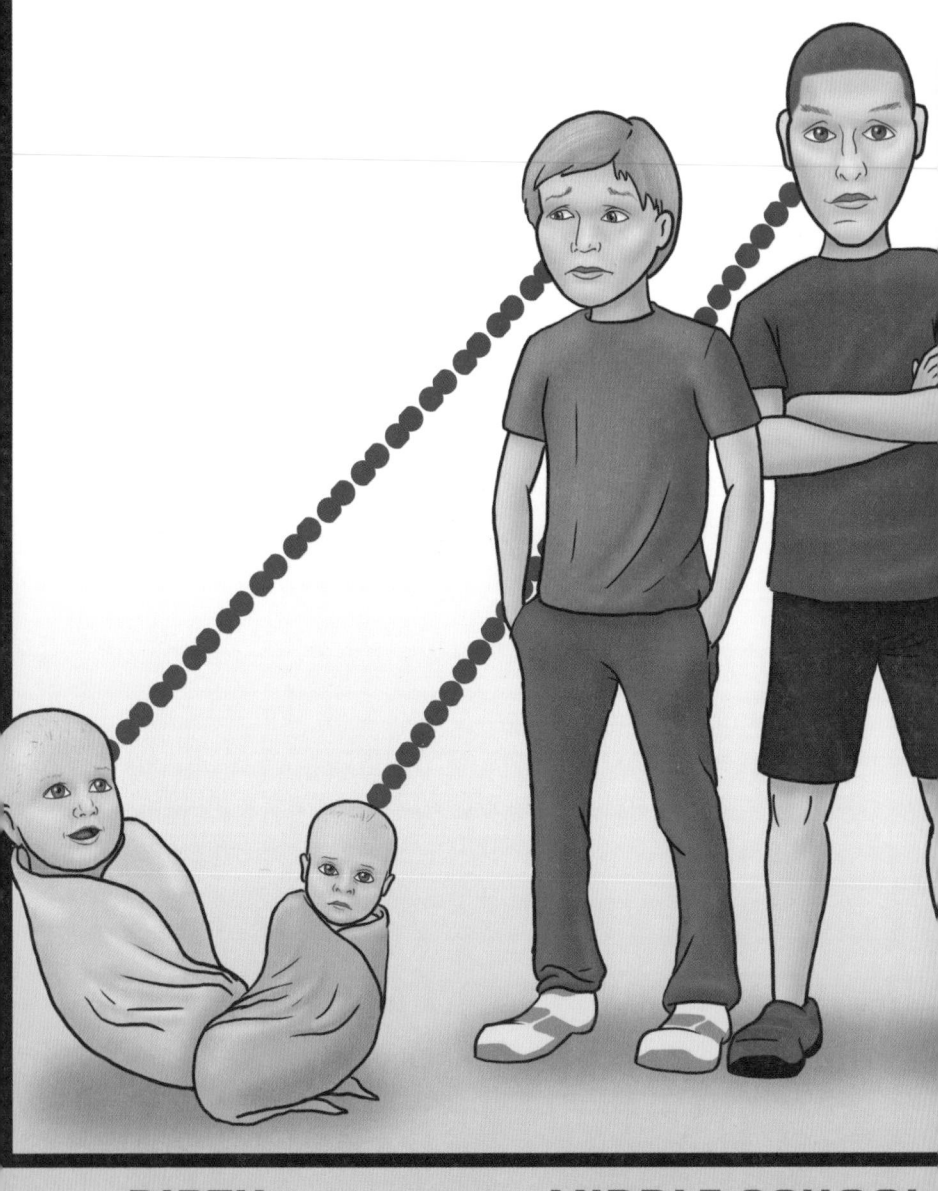

BIRTH   MIDDLE SCHOOL

Chapter 7

Struggling in Football

When he was born, Brian weighed 12 pounds—more than four pounds heavier than the average American baby boy. But in elementary and middle school, Brian was usually smaller than his male classmates.

He was 5 feet 8 inches and weighed 125 pounds before eighth grade football.

He wasn't the fastest player, but he always ran at full speed. He wasn't the strongest player, but he never shied away from contact. He was fearless.

Brian liked to take on bigger players.

Carlsbad, a town about an hour southwest of Lovington, had lots of towering players; a couple even had mustaches! There was a legendary tale that the kids from Carlsbad were so big because

there were special nutrients in the water that came out of the Pecos River.

Many of Brian's teammates were afraid.

Carlsbad didn't run a very complicated offense or defense. On offense, behind their big linemen, Carlsbad's shifty running back ran wherever he wanted. And on defense, Carlsbad's big linemen dominated Lovington's undersized front line.

But Brian wasn't intimidated.

Even though he didn't get much blocking from his teammates, Brian refused to give up on any play and willed his way into the end zone for a three-yard touchdown in the third quarter. Then, in the fourth quarter, he leveled a Carlsbad linebacker, clearing the way for Brandon to score from 10 yards out.

Carlsbad, though, won the game 42–14.

Needing more production from the team's offense, Brian was moved from fullback to receiver midway through the season. His

coaches recognized that he was very good at catching the football.

Since Brandon was the team's quarterback, he and Brian would practice a lot after school. In the street in front of Brandon's house, they'd make up plays and try them. Once in a while, they convinced a kid in the neighborhood to defend Brian on pass routes.

Brian loved going to Brandon's house. His mom always stocked the pantry with the best snacks, like Zebra Cakes®, Swiss Rolls, and Star Crunch Cosmic Snacks. And in the fridge, Brandon's mom had Coca-Cola!

This is great, Brian thought.

During games, Brian and Brandon started to connect for touchdowns. Their favorite play was "Red 88." Brian would sprint down the field as fast as he could, and Brandon would throw the ball down the field as far as he could.

There were also a few plays only Brian and Brandon knew, and they were based on colors.

After Brian started playing receiver, his team started scoring more points. But they still couldn't stop anyone from scoring on them.

By season's end, Brian's team was 0–6. They lost every game by at least two touchdowns. Brian's hard work as a receiver helped, but he decided he needed to become a better defender.

We can score all the points we want, Brian thought, *but we can't win if the other team always scores more.*

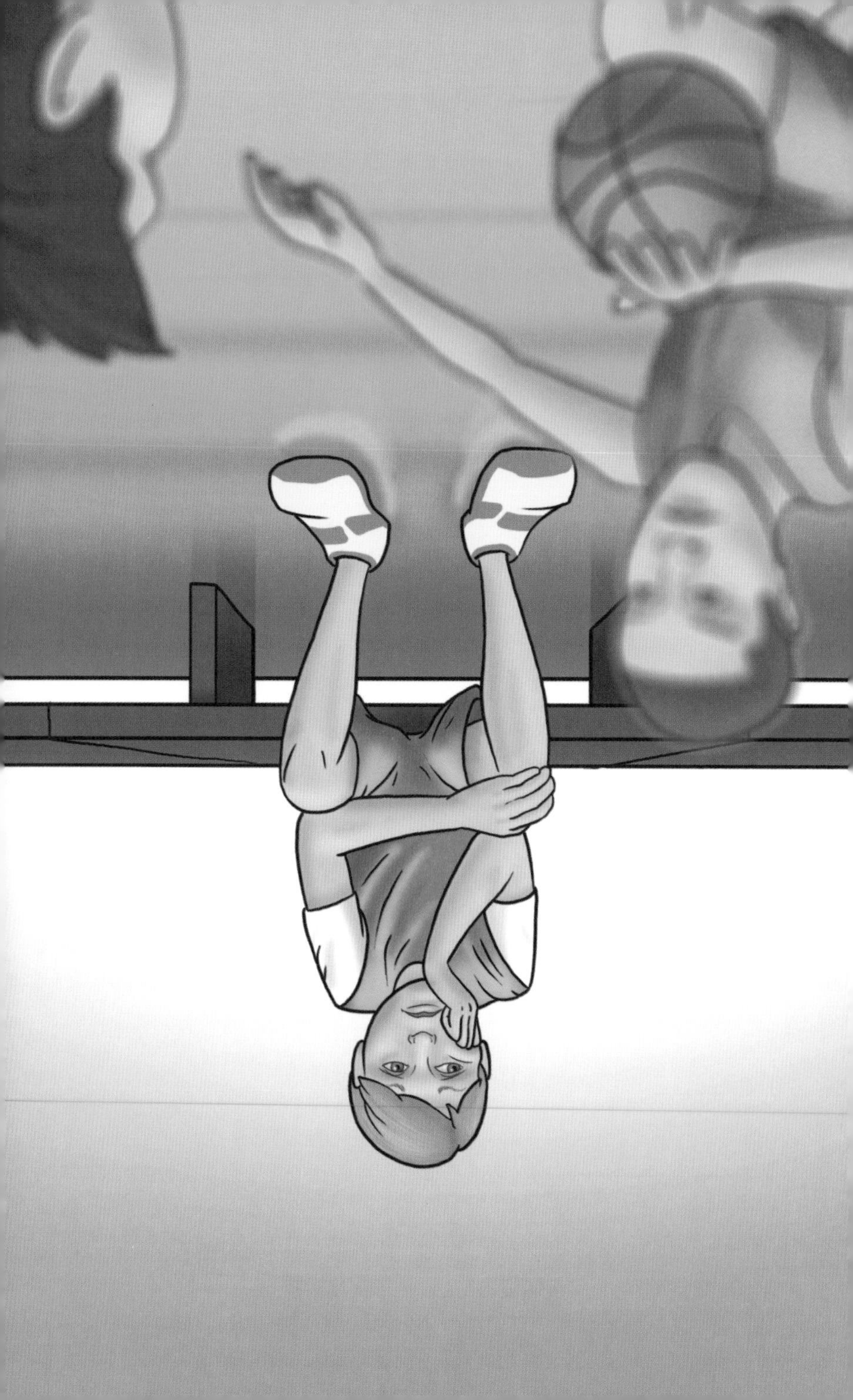

Chapter 8

Riding the Pine

After football season, Brian and Brandon transitioned to basketball. Both boys liked football, but they *loved* basketball.

Brandon was the team's star player, averaging 16 points per game. As point guard, he once scored 37 points in one game!

Brian, meanwhile, barely got off the bench. He wasn't the team's smallest player (that was John, who was 5 feet 2 inches), but Brian wasn't big enough to play in the paint, and he wasn't a very good dribbler, especially going to his left.

If Coach Black did play Brian, it was at the end of a game, when the outcome was already

45

determined. That's sometimes called "garbage time." Brian would get mad when Coach Black didn't play him, but he'd get even madder when he was on the court for garbage time.

"Coach Black doesn't know what he's doing," Brian would protest to Sheri, who was a star basketball player. "I know I can play, but he just doesn't give me a chance when it matters."

"Sounds like you're thinking of quitting, Brian," Sheri said. "You know what Mom thinks of that..."

"I'm not, Sheri," Brian responded. "It's just...it's just...so unfair!"

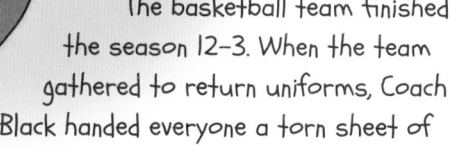

The basketball team finished the season 12–3. When the team gathered to return uniforms, Coach Black handed everyone a torn sheet of paper.

"Write the name of the team MVP on the paper and toss it into my hat," he said.

Brian immediately scribbled down Brandon's name and tossed the paper into Coach's hat. Coach Black tabulated the votes and everyone voted for Brandon...except for one person. Coach didn't say who cast that vote, but Brian couldn't wait to clear the air as he walked home with his best friend.

"You know I voted for you, Brandon," Brian blurted out as soon as they left the gym.

"I know, Brian," Brandon calmly said. "I didn't even think that; it was probably Jimmy."

Jimmy was the team's best interior player, and he led the team in blocked shots and rebounds.

"He probably voted for himself," Brandon jokingly said.

"Yeah, you're probably right," Brian replied.

"I don't care about that stuff, Brian; I just want to win. I got your back, and you got mine, right?"

Brian nodded and smiled.

When they got to Brandon's house, the boys celebrated with Zebra Cakes® and a Coke.

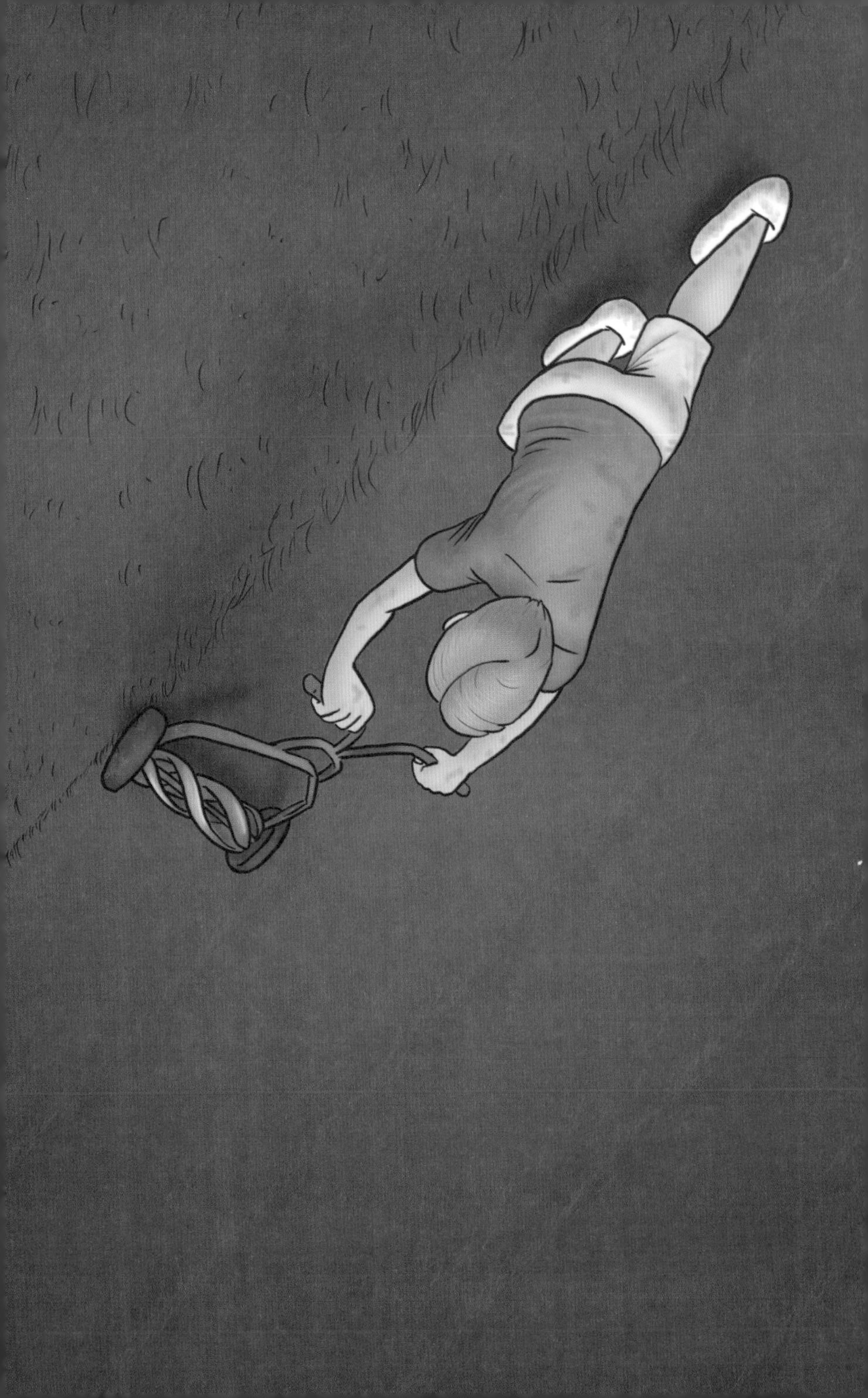

Chapter 9

Working for More

Brian's mom and step-dad both worked hard, waking up before the kids left for school and sometimes coming home after dinner. But they attended games, talked to teachers, and interacted with coaches.

In seventh grade, after Lovington High School hired Speedy Faith as its head football coach, Brian's mom pulled him aside. After a brief introduction, Brian's mom got right to the point.

"Speedy, I want us to start a mentoring program at the middle school," she told the new head coach. "The young boys look up to the high school football players in this town. Let me know what you want me to do, but I think our community needs this."

Coach Faith agreed, so he arranged for the varsity football players—during the season—to visit with the middle school boys once a week. Brian, of course, didn't know that his mom initiated the program, but he sure enjoyed hanging out with the football players! In Lovington, the high school football players were celebrities.

Except for the convenience and grocery stores, the town would almost shut down when the Wildcats played at home. The middle-school boys marveled at receiver John Cunningham, who had visited Texas Tech in Lubbock, Texas. Although it was in a different state, Lubbock was the closest major city to Lovington: about two hours away.

Lovington's home football games were jam-packed, with a capacity of 6,000 fans, and Brian and Brandon attended each one. Kids could get into the game for free, but the boys—like everyone else—had to buy snacks from the concession stand. Brian's mom and step-dad supported the family, but they didn't have a whole lot of extra money, especially for things like treats at a game. Those were luxuries, not necessities.

Brian, Casey, and Sheri didn't complain; they each picked up jobs to earn some spending money.

Walking home one day, Brian noticed their neighbors, the Fitzgeralds, loading their stuff into a big yellow moving truck.

"Where are you guys going?" Brian asked Jeremy, who was 10 years old.

"We're moving to Dallas," Jeremy said. "My dad got a new job."

"It was nice knowing ya!"

As he walked by their mailbox, Brian noticed a lawnmower among a heap of stuff. This lawnmower didn't have an engine; it had blades that rotated as it moved forward or backward.

"That's it!" Brian said aloud, even though he was by himself. "I'll mow lawns to make money!"

Brian walked around the whole neighborhood and told any adult he saw about his new business. He didn't have a name or anything, but he *kind of* had a uniform. He had an old pair of white shoes, a faded pair of blue shorts, and a light blue shirt.

Brian would lug his mower to anyone's house who wanted a fresh-cut lawn. After a while, he developed a reputation because he worked hard and he worked quickly.

"Oh Brian, how do you get such straight lines?" Mrs. Bradley, whose husband had died a few years earlier, would always ask him. She gave Brian extra cash for doing a good job!

The summer before ninth grade, Brian had made $80 mowing lawns.

Before school started in August, the town celebrated the Lee County Fair and Rodeo. It was THE EVENT for kids in town, with a merry-go-round and different games. The boys loved to play Pop-A-Shot. They would see who could rack up the most points in the rapid-fire, mini-basketball shooting game.

But the prizes were lame. The best

prizes were at the regulation basketball game.

It seemed like the whole eighth grade basketball team was there the first night of the fair, including Brandon. Brian's girlfriend Sally had her mind set on a stuffed cat because she collected them.

Stuffed animals were tough to win. For $1, you got five shots from the top of the key (a three-pointer). If you made three shots, you won a mini Spurs or Mavericks basketball. Four, and you won a medium-sized stuffed animal of your choice, including the cat Sally wanted. Make five and you would win a life-sized stuffed animal.

Brandon went first, and he nailed his first three shots. His fourth attempt hit the back of the rim then rattled out.

"Come on, Brandon!" Brian shouted as his friend lined up for his final shot.

Make it, and Brandon would win a stuffed animal. Miss it, and Brandon would get a mini basketball. Brandon swished his final shot and smiled as he handed his girlfriend Jennifer a medium-sized stuffed bird.

Three other teammates tried to win prizes but none of them could even make three. Jimmy proved why Coach Black didn't let him shoot threes in games. He failed to make a single shot.

It was Brian's turn to shoot.

Ever since the season ended, he had committed himself to improving. Brandon loved to work on his game too. Since his uncle, Chief, was Lovington's varsity basketball coach, Brandon was allowed to rebound, fetch balls, and fill water bottles when the big kids practiced. Then he'd get to practice in the school's sparkling gym when the high school kids had finished.

Brian always tagged along, and Chief gave Brian some pointers and drills so he could dribble with both hands and shoot better. Chief didn't see star potential in Brian, but he appreciated Brian's willingness to listen.

The Fair and Rodeo was the time for Brian's hard work to pay off.

He was nervous when the game attendant tossed him the first ball. Brian needed to impress Sally after all! He sent the first shot toward the basket, but it hit the front of the rim and dropped to the ground.

"Come on, Brian!" Brandon whispered just loud enough for his best friend to hear. "You can do this."

With the ball in his hands, he took a deep breath, and he lofted his next shot toward the basket.

Swish.

He got into a rhythm. Catch, shoot.

Swish.

Catch, shoot.

Swish.

The ball for his last shot came, and Brian bobbled it. He collected himself, took a deep breath then launched it. The ball sailed through the air and hit the back of the rim, then it shot up toward the clouds. Everyone gasped as the ball seemed to move in slow motion. When it came down, it splashed right through the net.

"Yeah, I get my cat!" Sally squealed.

Brian smiled as Brandon gave him a fist bump.

There were more games, like throwing balls at plates, and lots and lots of treats like cotton candy.

After a while, Sally started to get very quiet.

"What's wrong?" Brian asked her.

"Well, I like this cat," she said, "but I saw the bigger cat you could win at the basketball shooting game. Can you win me that one?"

Brian sighed.

They walked back toward the game, and Brian got in line. When his turn came, Brian realized he didn't have any money left. He had spent all $80!

"Sorry, Sally. I'm all out," Brian sheepishly said, turning the pockets of his shorts inside out.

Brian still had a night he wouldn't soon forget.

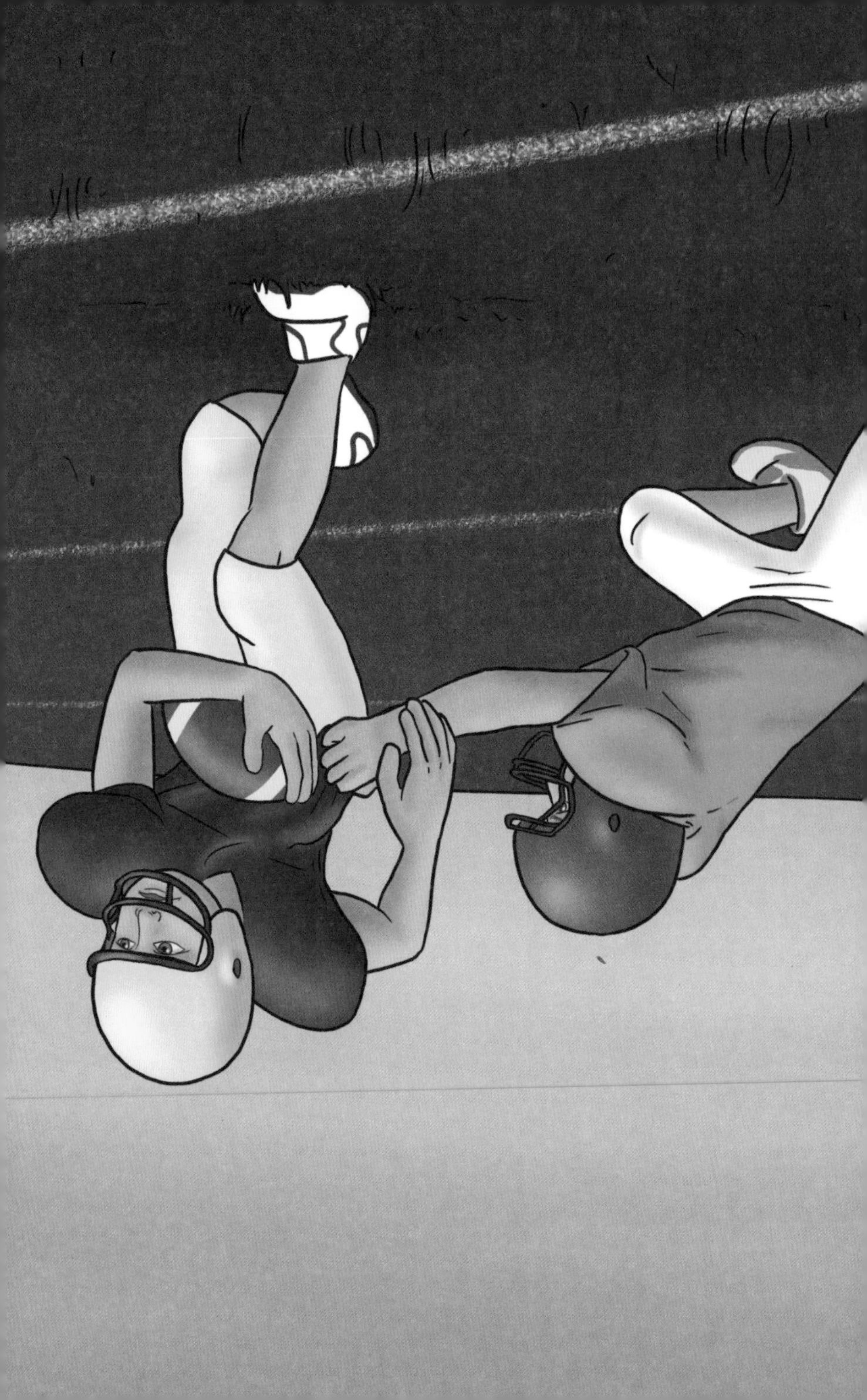

Chapter 10

The Close Call

Brian and Brandon were certain their ninth grade football team would be better than it was in eighth grade. After all, they couldn't be worse (0–6).

They practiced a lot and added to their playbook. Their favorite was a trick play. Brandon would take the snap and quickly toss it to Brian, who would take a step backward. (That's called a lateral, because the ball is behind the line of scrimmage.) As all the defenders would run toward Brian, Brandon would sneak to the far sideline. When the defenders neared Brian, he would throw the ball across the field to Brandon...who would be wide open.

At least that's how it always played out when they practiced it.

Before their first game, Brian's coach decided his players needed to scrimmage another team. Brian was nervous when he found out the opponent: Lovington's eighth grade football team, led by his little brother Casey.

Brian's teammates were confident they could beat the eighth graders, but Brian knew something few others did about Casey; he was tough *and* talented. When they were younger, Brian and Casey would wrestle often. But Brian didn't like to wrestle anymore because Casey was getting really strong—maybe even stronger than Brian was.

Casey was a fullback, and he was hard to stop. And, like his older brother, Casey was a fearless defender.

Brian knew his team had a worthy opponent, regardless of the age difference.

The eighth grade team got the ball first, and they quickly moved the ball down the field with Casey picking up four or five yards every time he ran it. Even if a defender got to Casey after a yard or two, Casey was strong enough to plow his way to an extra few yards. On his touchdown run, he carried two defenders into the end zone for a four-yard touchdown.

Brian usually didn't get nervous during a game, but he felt nervous this time. He imagined the torture Casey would put him through if the eighth graders defeated the ninth graders.

On their first series, the ninth grade team had a third-and-two, but Brandon decided to call an audible—which means he changed the play. Instead of a run play, he attempted a pass to Brian. Brandon got hit as he threw, and the ball harmlessly bounced off one of his teammates.

The ninth grade team had to punt.

Now the ninth graders knew what Brian did all along: Casey wasn't afraid of them.

Through the years, Casey had to survive scuffles with his older sister and his older brother. That's not uncommon for kids with older siblings. Younger siblings have a choice to make: Accept that fate, or fight back.

Casey always fought back.

Casey's team had a third-and-short, and they called a dive—a straightforward run. Brian burst up the middle, and he slammed into Casey for a one-yard loss.

In the huddle, Brandon told his teammates, "Sorry about my last throw. Let's get that ball in the end zone."

Brandon completed three straight passes to Brian, including a 25-yard touchdown pass.

The game was tied.

Since it wasn't a real game, the coaches said that each team would get one more possession.

Casey carried his team down the field again, but his quarterback threw a third-down pass way over his receiver's head. Then the eighth grade kicker missed a 19-yard field goal.

Brandon took over, running the ball himself to get his team to midfield. Then he completed a slant pass to Brian for 22 yards. After a few more runs, the ninth graders only had three seconds left. They called a timeout, and they had to attempt a 24-yard field goal.

Brian and Brandon's friend Daniel handled the kicks, and he was really good in practice. Daniel also played soccer, so he had a powerful leg. He stepped up and drilled the kick. He pushed it right, but the ball hit the upright and bounced through the posts for a field goal.

The ninth graders had won!

"Whew...that was close," Brian said to Brandon on the sideline.

Brian was usually excited whenever his team won. But after this one, he was more relieved. Always a good sport, Brandon jogged over to Casey, giving him a high-five and a hug.

"Geez, Casey," Brandon said. "You're a really good player!"

"Great game."

Casey appreciated Brandon's encouragement, but he was still bitter about the loss. He really wanted to beat the ninth graders—and his big brother Brian.

"I'll get him next time," Casey said to himself, fighting back tears.

Seeing how upset his little brother was, Brian wanted to make him feel better.

"You played a great game, Casey," Brian said. "Come on. Let me buy you a Coke."

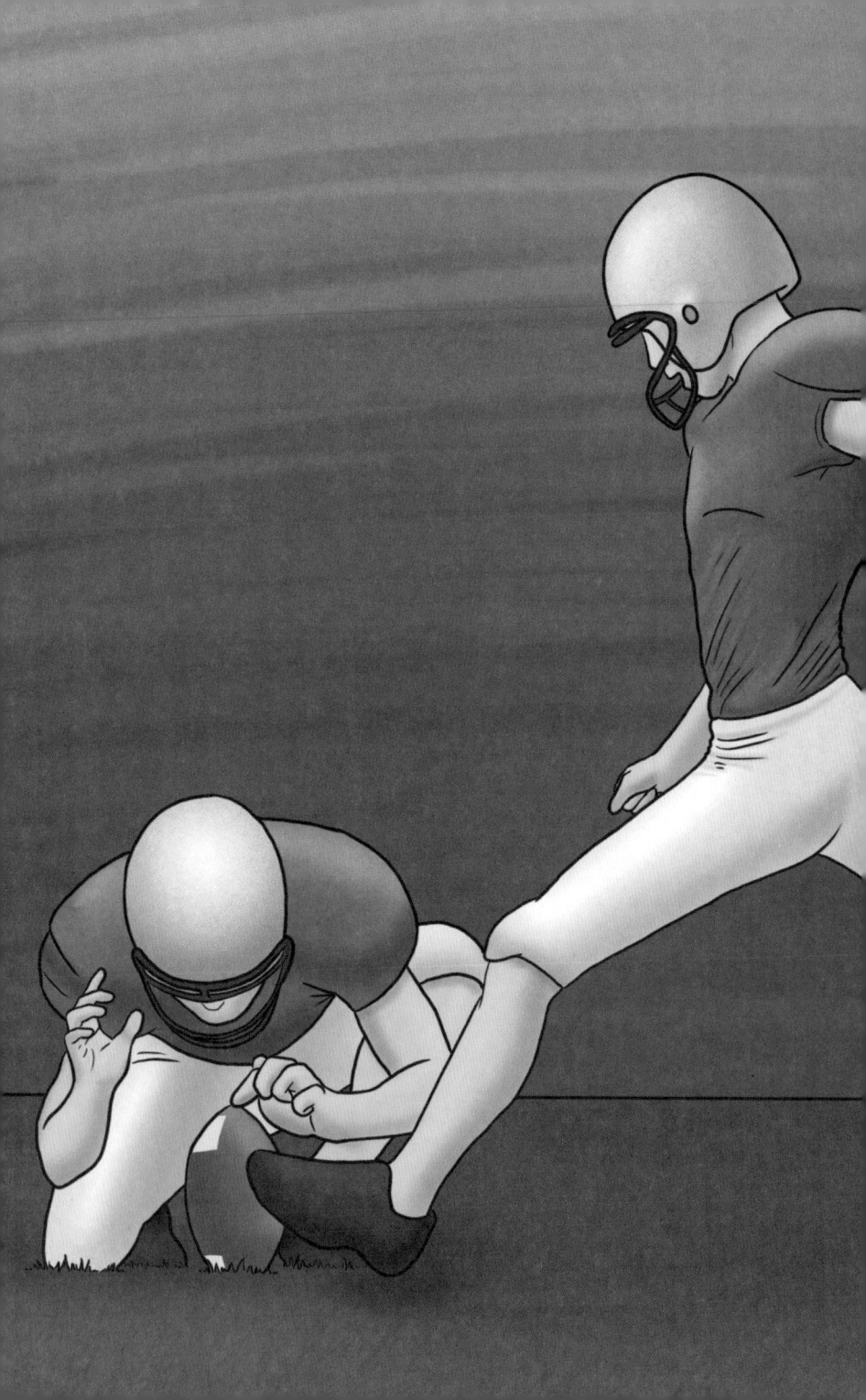

Chapter 11

We Are the Champions!

Victory—even against younger players—was short-lived for Brian's ninth grade football team. They lost their first three real games by big margins. They were scoring points, but their defense was still outsized and outmatched.

Roswell, a town about 90 minutes away, was supposed to play Lovington in the fourth game, but Roswell's bus broke down on U.S. Route 380, and they had to forfeit. That was Brian and Brandon's first win in football.

It didn't feel like a win, though, because they were dressed and warmed up before Coach huddled up and explained what happened.

The ninth graders lost a few more games, and Brian's teammates were frustrated. But nobody quit. They practiced hard, and they hung out at each other's houses a lot.

The worst part for Brian, though, was the fact that Casey's team was better—and his little brother made sure everyone knew it.

"Hey Brian, did your team win today?" Casey would ask at dinner.

"No," Brian would mumble between bites.

"That's too bad, Brian," Casey would say with a serious face.

"Guess what, Mom?" he'd say excitedly. "We won another game!"

Casey's eighth grade team finished their season 6-1.

Brian's final game was against Carlsbad. He wanted to win. Carlsbad had spanked Lovington 42–14 in eighth grade.

Brian and Brandon got into a rhythm. Carlsbad was bigger and faster, but Brandon and Brian kept connecting. At halftime, Lovington trailed 24–21.

No one kept statistics, but Brian definitely had over 100 receiving yards at halftime, and he'd scored every touchdown. In the third quarter, Brandon called "Red 88." Brian ran down the left sideline as fast as he could, and Brandon threw the ball as far as he could. Brandon hit Brian in stride.

"Go Brian, go BRIAN!" his mother screamed from the sidelines.

Brian was ahead of his defender, and he scored a 55-yard touchdown. Brandon sprinted down the middle of the field and hugged Brian in the end zone. With two minutes left, the game was tied 38–38.

"We got this," Brian said to himself, as he lined up on defense.

Brian seemed to be everywhere, tackling the Carlsbad's running back on first down, and sacking the quarterback on third down.

On offense, Brandon scrambled for a few first downs and hooked up with Brian for a 15-yard catch. But on third down, Brian got his legs tangled up with his defender, and he fell down as Brandon's throw sailed past him.

Daniel, the kicker, trotted onto the field for a 30-yard field goal. Brandon, who was the holder, looked into Daniel's eyes and nodded. Brian was one of the blockers on the kick. The snap wasn't very good, but Brandon quickly snatched the off-target ball and set it down. Daniel calmly went through his routine as he'd done dozens of times in practice. He kicked the ball perfectly to give his team a 41–38 lead.

"Yes!" Brandon said, as he pumped his fist and hugged Daniel.

"Good kick, dude," Brian said to Daniel, giving him a high five.

Now it was the defense's turn to hold again.

Brian's team had really struggled with defense all season, and they'd already given up 38 points. Carlsbad had a running back named Isaiah who was super fast. He shredded Lovington's defense, running behind his big offensive line. But after they got to midfield, they didn't have any more timeouts and there were only 25 seconds left.

The game was in the hands of Carlsbad's quarterback, who didn't have a very good arm. He also looked nervous—which is why his first three passes of the drive were way off target.

Then on fourth down, he chucked the ball about 25 yards down the field for Isaiah, but Brian swatted the ball down.

Lovington held on for the win!

After they shook hands with Carlsbad's players, Brian's teammates huddled up, jumped up and down, and yelled, "We did it!"

On the bus ride home, Coach had the driver play "We Are the Champions" by Queen over and over. It had been a rough season, but the boys were proud to beat a very good team on the road.

On the 90-minute bus ride back to Lovington on US-62, Brian dozed off and daydreamed about the future. What if he could play football in college? He could make his mother proud and earn a scholarship to play football at Texas Tech, which was close enough for his mother to drive to home games.

More than 50,000 would attend the Red Raiders' games! Plus, they had really cool black and red uniforms.

Brian even dared to dream about playing in the NFL. With his first big contract, he would buy his mom a new car and house so she wouldn't have to work—let alone at two or three different jobs—anymore.

A shout awoke Brian before he dreamed about playing in his first NFL game.

"Brian, we're here," Brandon said, shaking his friend. The bus had arrived in the high school parking lot.

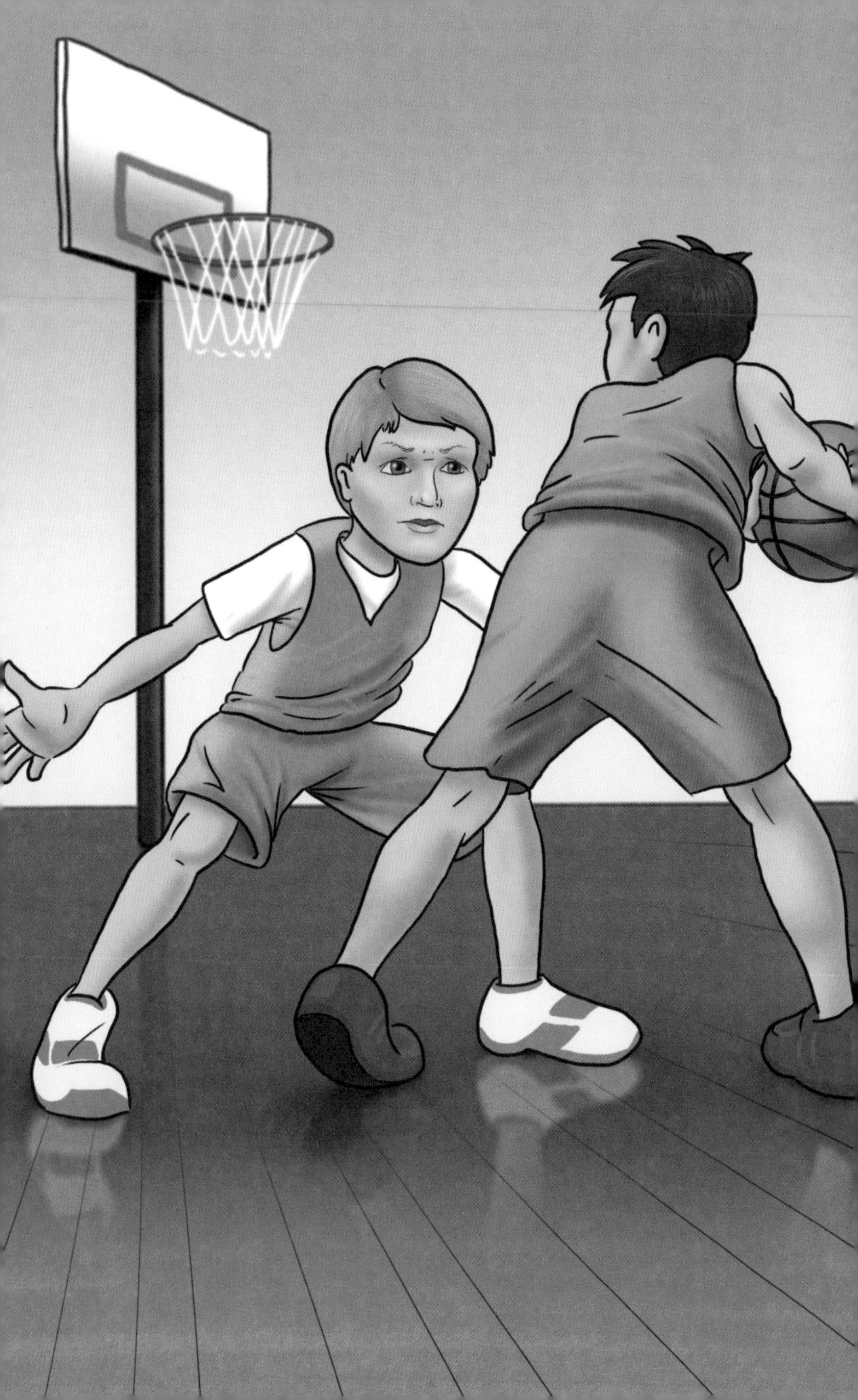

Chapter 12

Getting Into the Game

Brian was getting stronger, but he wasn't getting bigger. He and Casey would track their height behind their bedroom door.

"One inch?" Brian said disappointed.

That's all he'd grown between eighth and ninth grade.

"It's OK, little brother," Sheri mockingly said, emphasizing the word *little*. "At least you're not shrinking."

Casey laughed.

After football season,

Brian was excited to play his favorite sport. Besides, Coach Black wouldn't be running this team, so Brian was certain he'd play more.

He was right.

Plus, his hard work in the offseason had paid off.

Brian was the sixth man, which meant he was the first player to come off the bench. He usually would replace the shooting guard or small forward because Brandon never came off the court. Brandon was still the team's best player—by a long shot. He led the team in scoring, assists, and steals, and he was even second to Jimmy in rebounds.

Coach Bennett liked the way Brian played defense and often assigned him to defend the opponent's best guard. Brian embraced his role. What he lacked in size, he made up for in heart, chasing down loose balls, picking off passes, and going into the paint to grab a few rebounds.

His season-high in a single game was 10 points. But Brian averaged two-and-a-half steals a game, trailing only Brandon on the team.

After the team finished 11-4, Brian's mom congratulated him for all his hard work.

"Great job this season," she told him on the drive home after his final game. "Your game really improved!"

In the back seat, sitting in his sweatpants and sweatshirt, Brian smiled and thanked her. Then he got a surprise.

"Mom's right, Brian," Sheri chimed in. "You did get a lot better… but you still can't shoot, and you still can't beat me."

Brian smiled. That was as close to a compliment as Sheri handed out.

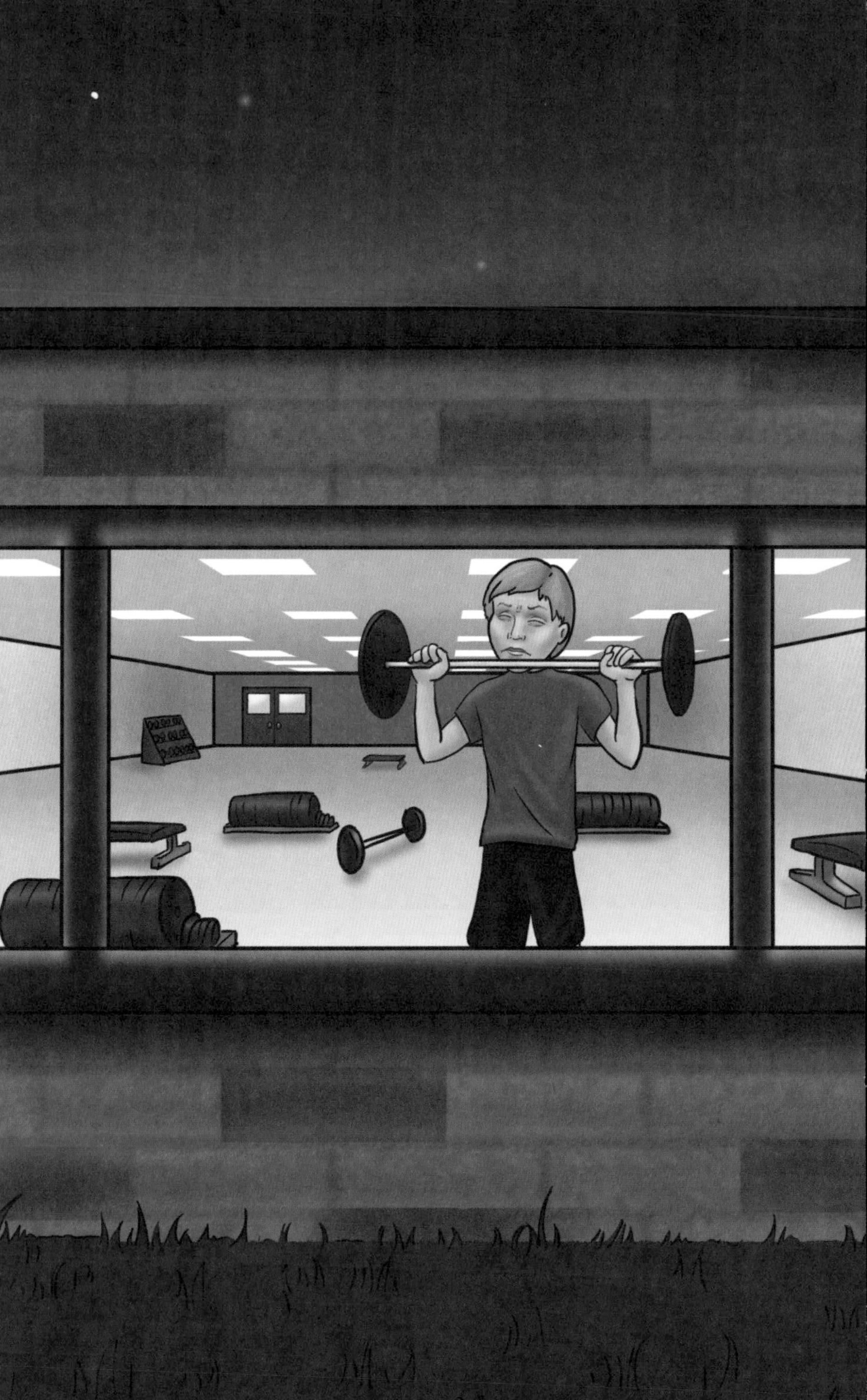

Chapter 13

Early Morning Workouts

In the spring, before the junior varsity season, Coach Quinones—everyone called him Coach Q—addressed all the football players.

"Guys, if we're going to be successful, everyone's got to get stronger," he said. "We can't keep letting these big schools push us around."

Coach Q was the strength coach and he worked with the defensive backs. The varsity players usually lifted weights after practice, but he announced that he would open up the weight room *before* school.

Brian was very excited.

He did 100 pushups and 200 sit-ups every day, but he really liked the dumbbells and barbells in the weight room. He liked the soundtrack of the weight room: a mix of rock and rap music and the clanking of weights.

When the first football meeting was over, Brian noticed that Brandon wasn't there. He rushed over to Brandon's house and knocked on the door.

Brandon, who was holding a Swiss Roll, answered.

"How come you weren't at the meeting?" Brian asked.

"I decided I don't want to play football anymore," Brandon said. "It's a lot of work, and I'm tired of losing all the time. I'm going to focus on basketball."

Brian was heartbroken.

That night at dinner Brian asked his mom and step-dad if he could attend the early-morning workouts with Coach Q.

"I think that's a good idea," Troy said.

"Can I come? Can I come?" Casey asked.

Before Brian could answer, Troy added, "I think

that's a good idea too."

Most kids didn't like to get up early, but Brian and Casey didn't mind; they usually went to bed around nine anyway. And Troy left early for work, so they could hitch a ride to the school with him.

At the first workout, though, only five players showed up: Brian, Casey, Mark, and the varsity co-captains Rich Longfellow and James Johnson. Coach Q seemed sad about the turnout, but he handed each of them a sheet of paper with lots of boxes.

"This is so you can track your progress," he told the players.

Coach Q opened up the weight room at 5 a.m. Only Brian, Casey, and Mark showed up every day.

One day, during a break, the boys noticed Coach Q cleaning up a dusty old chalkboard.

"Coach, what are you doing?" Brian asked him.

"I'm writing in the record holders for the weight room," Coach Q said. "I had to do some digging, but I found out all the Wildcats who have done the most bench presses, deadlifts, squats, and power cleans."

"I want those records," Casey said quietly to himself.

Brian heard his brother—and he recognized something very quickly; although he was older, Casey seemed stronger. Brian couldn't accept that, so he committed himself to working harder in the weight room.

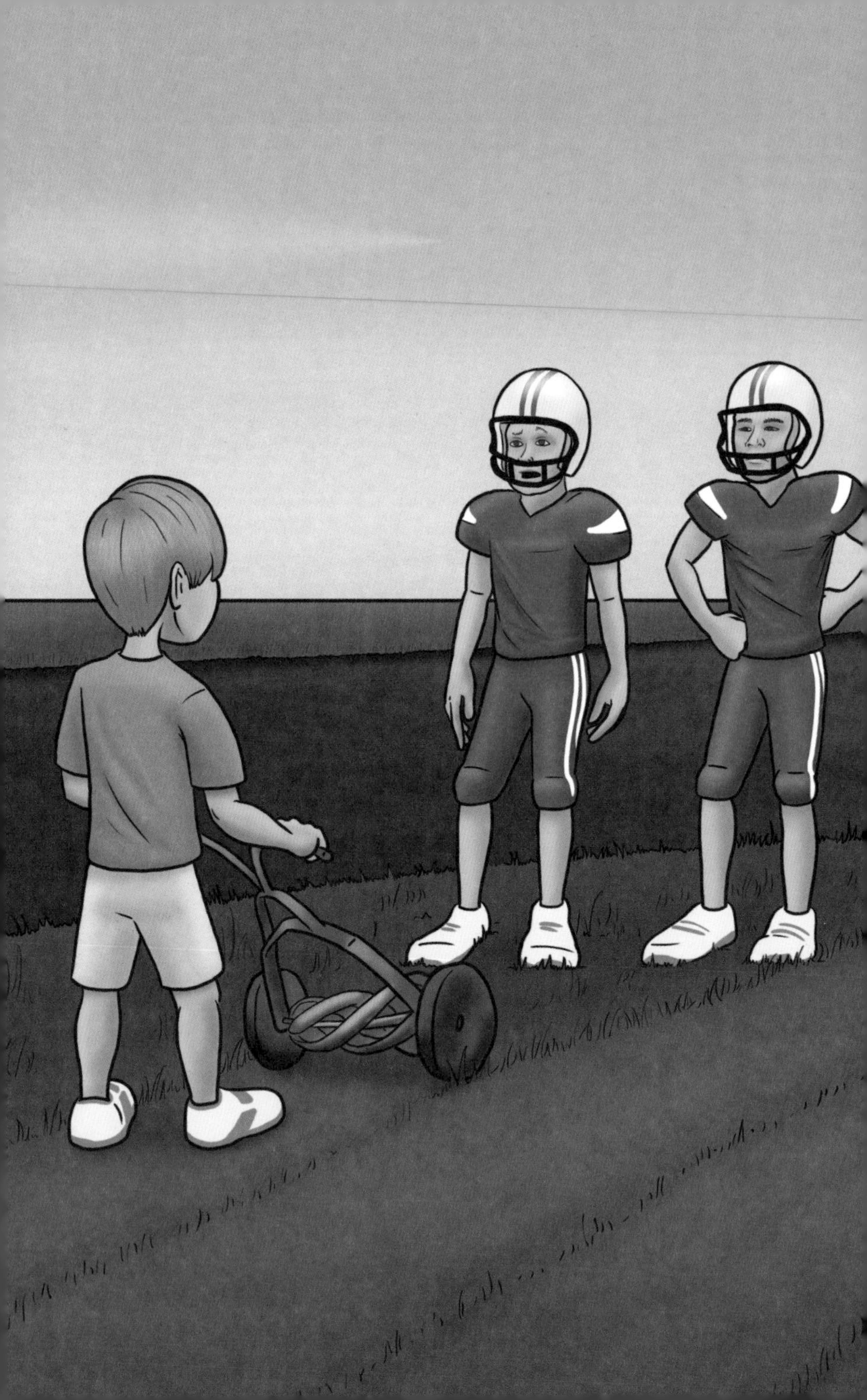

Chapter 14

"Where's Brian?"

Over the summer, Brian and Casey continued to be regulars at Coach Q's early morning workouts. When he could, Brian would convince his JV teammates to join him. But a few guys would only show up a day or two each week, if at all.

Brian hadn't grown much, but he loved watching himself get stronger and stronger in the weight room. Still, he just couldn't out-lift his little brother in anything.

Casey made it all look so easy, especially the bench press and squat. The bench press is when you lay on an exercise bench, lower a barbell with plates, and lift it back up. Each lowering and lifting of the barbell and plates is called a repetition.

The school record for the bench press was 35 repetitions of 225 pounds set in 1985 by Jim "Beast" Benson. Casey wanted that record. So, naturally, Brian did too.

Brian could do more than any of the other guys who showed up, but Casey could do the most. He could do 18 repetitions. Brian was at 16.

Since they were often the only two who showed up, Brian and Casey had to spot for each other. That means one would be there to help the other in case they couldn't lift the barbell because they were too tired.

It was tough on Brian because he had to practice in the late morning right after weight training. On the first day of training camp, Brian was exhausted after his workout and practice. He didn't want to, but he had committed to mowing a neighbor's lawn that afternoon. He really wanted the cash, so he didn't even bother showering after practice and jogged home to grab his mower.

At 3:30 p.m., though, Coach Faith noticed Brian wasn't around.

"Where's Urlacher?" Coach said.

No one said anything.

During training camp, the Wildcats practiced *twice* a day, once in the morning and once in the afternoon.

Coach Faith asked again, "Where's Urlacher?"

One teammate quietly said, "Uh, he's across the street mowing Mr. Allen's lawn."

At Mr. Allen's, Brian was half finished when he noticed a sea of teammates in blue jerseys walking down Avenue C toward him.

"What are you guys doing?" Brian asked.

"Coach sent us to get you," Mark said. "He wants you to know that we've got football practice, and we can't continue without you."

Brian turned red, embarrassed that 20-plus players—in their helmets and cleats—were sent to retrieve him. He wanted to make money, but he also wanted to be a good teammate. He prided himself on satisfying his customers, and Mr. Allen wanted his lawn mowed before he got home from work.

What should I do? Brian thought. His teammates were waiting.

Brian left his mower in Mr. Allen's yard, hustled back to the high school, and suited up for practice. If he hurried, Brian could get back to Mr. Allen's before he got home.

All that, though, would have to wait. When Brian sprinted

toward the field, Coach Faith was waiting for him.

"I know you're trying to make some money," Coach said, "but you made a commitment to me and this team. You'll have plenty of time this summer to mow lawns. Now give me four laps."

Brian had mixed emotions as he ran. School hadn't started, and Brian wanted to make and save money. His family could only afford the essentials, and he knew he'd need some cash for snacks, movie tickets, and fast-food outings with his friends. But he was also flattered that Coach Faith cared and noticed he *wasn't* at practice, and that he needed to be with his teammates so they could grow together.

With so much racing through his mind, Brian breezed through his four laps and prepared to rejoin practice.

But Coach Faith had another idea: "Now give me 50 push-ups, Urlacher!"

In Lovington, students attended the high school for grades 10 through 12.

Just when he started to understand middle school rules, Brian had to get ready for high school. What new rules would Brian have to learn on the field and in his life?

He wasn't sure, but he was eager to find out.

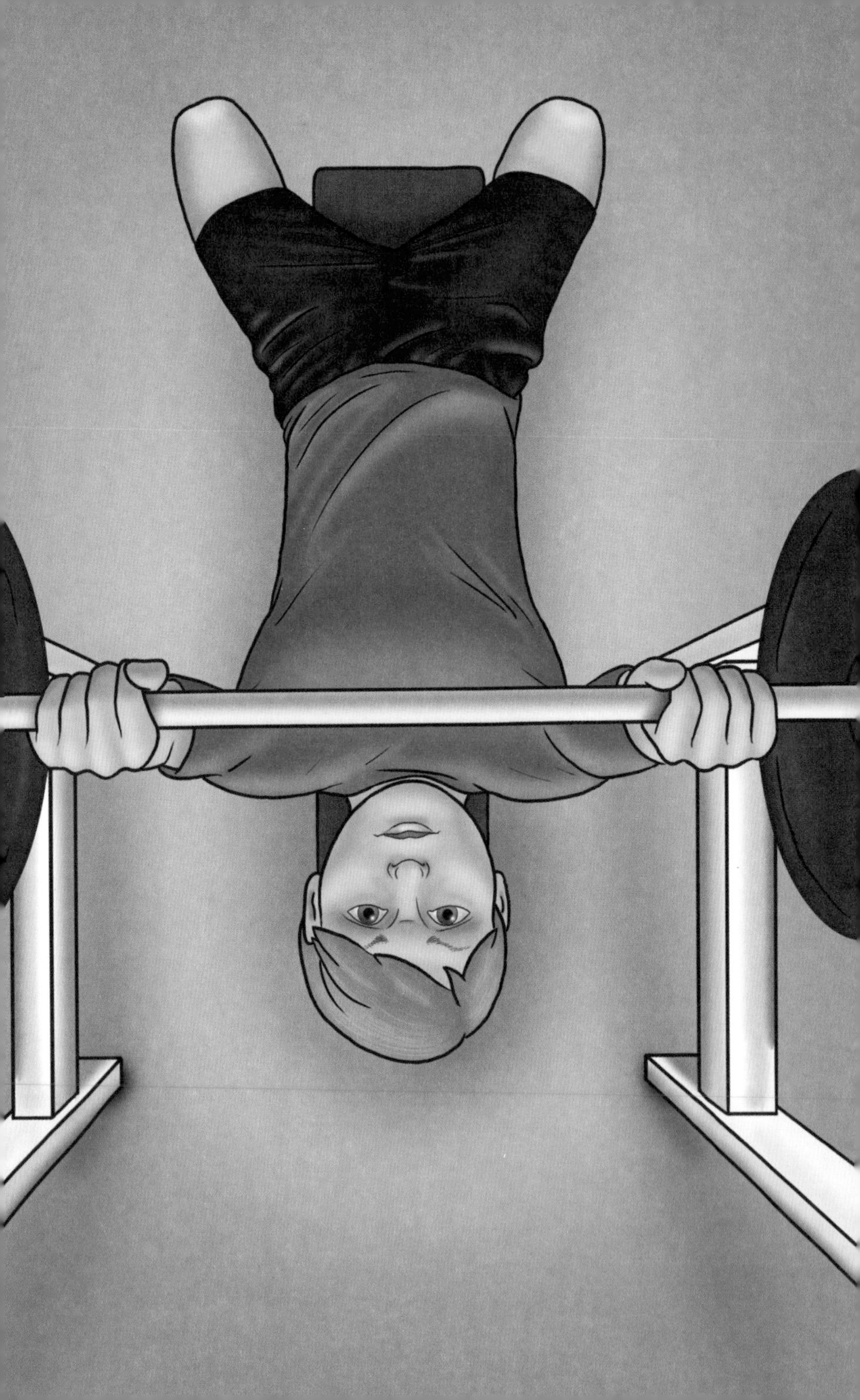

Chapter 15

Turning the Corner

Brian was excited for junior varsity football. He still wasn't tall, but he wasn't skinny anymore. He was 5 feet, 11 inches, and he weighed 165 pounds.

Coach Bryant told Brian he would play receiver on offense and safety on defense. But who was going to throw him the ball? With Brandon not playing, the JV team needed a quarterback.

During training camp, Coach Bryant had an open tryout for anyone interested in playing the position. Only two players showed interest: Stevie Edwards and Ricky Johnson. Ricky was Brandon's backup in ninth grade.

He was the starting running back, so he was fast, but Ricky couldn't throw the ball very well. Stevie, on the other hand, was one of the slowest players on the team, but he had a really good arm. He could throw the ball further than anyone else could—including Brandon.

Give Stevie time and he could usually get the ball where it needed to go. Unfortunately, the 10th graders never had very good offensive linemen.

Brian continued his early morning workouts with Coach Q, and he decided he needed some of his JV teammates to show up too. After two long practices, as players gathered their pads and helmets, Brian told his teammates to show up outside the weight room early the next morning.

"No way!" several players said.

"That's too early," another said.

"I'm already too tired from two practices a day!" one teammate added.

Brian wasn't one to say a whole lot, but he was really tired of losing all the time.

"Look, if you guys want to keep getting pounded by other teams, then let's not change anything," he calmly said. "But if we're going to turn things around, we've got to get stronger. I'll be there at 5 a.m.," Brian added, heading for the exit.

The next morning, Troy was running just a few minutes behind schedule. He dropped Brian and Casey off at the gym at 5:03 a.m.

Ah man, no one else showed up, Brian thought. But when he

opened the door to the weight room, he heard the clanging of weights and bass pumping from the cheap speakers on the walls.

Eight of his JV teammates had shown up!

"Where you been, Urlacher?" Stevie joked. "We started without ya."

Brian's JV team opened the 1993 season against Eunice High School. Eunice was a smaller town, about 48 miles south of Lovington. They had one of the best baseball programs in the state. But they also were pretty solid in football.

Stevie was nervous before his first JV game. In fact, he looked like he was going to be sick.

"You all right, Stevie?" Brian asked.

"I'm not feeling so great," Stevie quietly said. "I don't know if I can do this."

Brian knew that his teammate was nervous to start his first game as quarterback in front of a couple hundred people. Brian didn't know what to say, so he said the first thing that popped into his head.

"Stevie, just concentrate on me and don't worry about anyone else. Let's get a couple completions, and you'll be just fine."

Brian knew he had to help Stevie. Brian would have to work extra hard to get open early in the game. By creating more space between himself and his defender, Brian would give Stevie an easier pass to attempt. That would help build Stevie's confidence.

Brian made sure he and Stevie were on the same page in the

huddle, and then Brian focused on his route-running and catching passes cleanly.

On Lovington's first offensive series, Stevie completed three of four passes for 45 yards—all of them to Brian. The final pass was an eight-yarder that Brian dove for.

"Great job, Brian!" his mother yelled. "Keep it up!"

On the next series, Lovington's offense got Ricky, their running back, involved. So when they headed to halftime, up 17–6, Stevie seemed downright comfortable.

Coach Bryant wanted Ricky to run the ball more in the second half.

Lovington cruised to a 30–13 win.

Brian's team was undefeated! They even won their next two games, starting the season 3–0. Brian was really pumped. He'd never had this much success in football.

But then Brian got into some trouble.

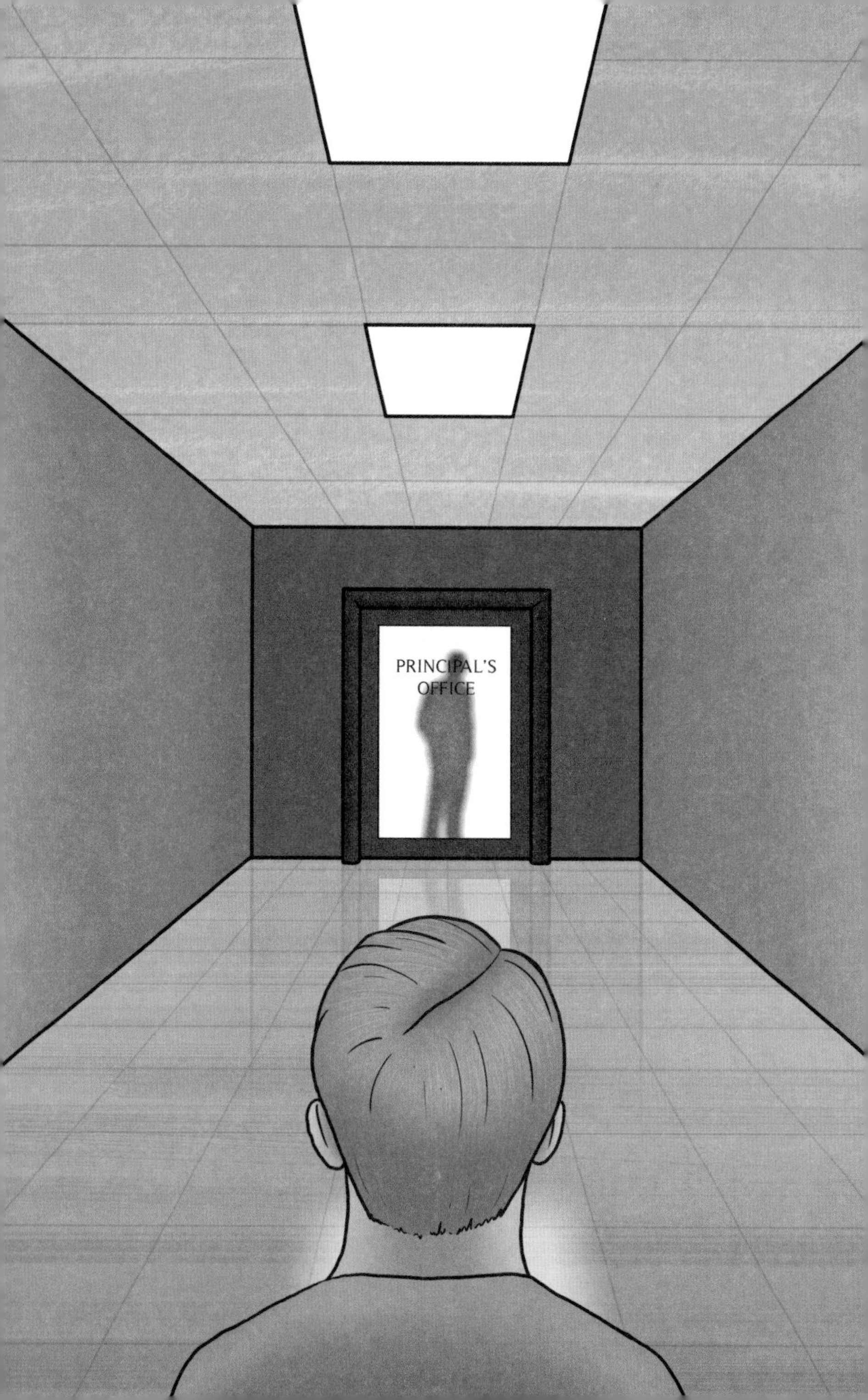
PRINCIPAL'S
OFFICE

Chapter 16

Principal Karger

It was the day of the big game against Hobbs, a town just a half hour away. Brian and a few buddies were in Ms. Wheeler's Algebra class before lunchtime. Brian and Daniel were the last two to leave class. They were laughing as they entered the hallway and passed Ms. Wheeler, who had excused herself just before class ended to go to the bathroom.

After stopping by his locker, Brian headed to the long line in the lunchroom. Before he could even put any of the spaghetti on his tray, Principal Karger walked up to him and pulled him out of line.

"Come with me," Principal Karger said.

"Ooohhhh," a few people said quietly in unison.

Brian knew this wasn't good. Principal Karger was tough and strict. When he got to Principal Karger's office, Brian saw Ms. Wheeler and Daniel.

"After you boys left the classroom, I noticed the answer pages for our next test were ripped out of my binder," Ms. Wheeler said. "Where are they?"

Brian was confused.

"I have no idea," Brian said before pausing. "Wait...you think I took them?"

Daniel didn't say anything. He just kept his head down.

No one said a word for what seemed like forever.

Principal Karger broke the silence.

"Ms. Wheeler says one of you boys took her answers. Now fess up, and you won't get in as much trouble."

Daniel was still silent.

Brian was slowly getting angry; his mind was racing. He knew he hadn't done anything wrong. Besides, math was one of his best classes; he wasn't tempted to cheat, and he didn't need to.

"I haven't done anything wrong," Brian sternly said.

"Do you boys know what that is?" Principal Karger said, pointing to a two-foot board. The board looked like Uncle Henry—Troy's tool for doling out punishment at Brian's house.

Of his siblings, Brian had the fewest run-ins with Uncle Henry, and he had never been in the principal's office before. He was concerned, but he wasn't afraid. He was defiant because he hadn't done anything wrong.

"If you boys don't admit that you took the answers, we're going to have a real problem," Principal Karger said. "Brian, aren't you supposed to play in a football game tonight?"

Brian looked up, wondering where Principal Karger was going with this.

"Well, if you don't tell me the truth, then you're not going to play against Hobbs," Principal Karger said.

Now Brian was really mad. He looked Principal Karger in the eyes and said again, "I haven't done anything wrong."

"If you boys aren't going to own up to this, then you have a choice," Principal Karger continued. "Take two swats from that board, or be suspended from all activities—including tonight's football game—for a week. Your choice."

It was a no-brainer for Brian.

Sure, he was mad that he was accused of doing something he hadn't done, and he was being unfairly punished, but he figured the pain was momentary compared to missing a whole game.

Two swats instead of four quarters.

So Brian stood up and said, "I'll take the swats."

Without hesitation, Principal Karger grabbed the two-foot board, and Brian turned around.

Smack!

Brian was startled at how suddenly and strongly Principal Karger struck him in the behind with the board. Before he could even regroup, Brian was struck again.

Smack!

The second blow was even harder, causing Brian to take a small leap forward to keep his balance. His backside hurt, but Brian certainly wasn't going to give anyone the satisfaction of seeing him cry.

Instead, he looked Principal Karger in the eyes again and said, "Are we done?"

Principal Karger nodded, and Brian walked toward the exit.

Once he got back in the hallway, Brian let the incident go. He had been punished for something he didn't do, but he didn't want his pride to stop him from doing what he loved and being there with his teammates.

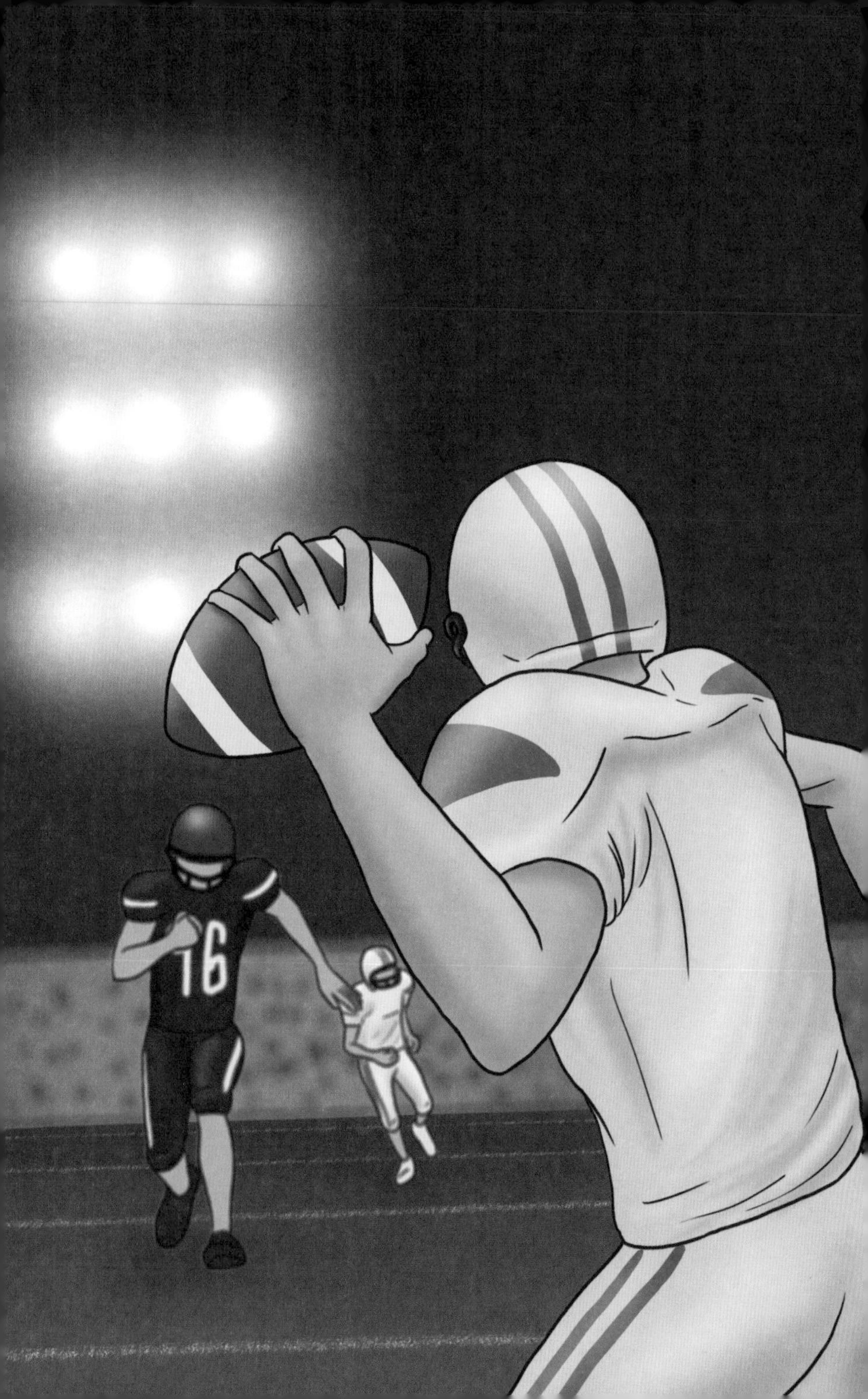
16

Chapter 17

Dealing With a Tough Loss

Brian was ready to dish out his own punishment against Hobbs. Hobbs didn't have a very good offense, but they had a really good defense.

Brian's teammates had gotten stronger because of the extra weight lifting sessions, but they still couldn't match up with Hobbs' defensive linemen. Not only were Hobbs' players powerful, they were also fast. Stevie had no time to set up in the pocket behind the line of scrimmage. Stevie didn't move that well, and he got sacked and drilled throughout the first quarter.

He attempted three passes and all of them were way off target. The fourth one was intercepted and returned 58 yards for a touchdown.

The game was a frustrating one for Brian. As a receiver, he couldn't contribute if he couldn't get the ball, and Stevie just wasn't giving Brian a chance to make any plays.

By halftime, Brian had only one catch for six yards. His team trailed 17-0.

Brian's team did a little better in the second half, with Brian returning the opening kickoff for a touchdown and forcing a fumble later in the third quarter. But Brian's team ended up losing the game 23-13.

They had lost their first game of the season.

That capped one of worst days of his life, as far as Brian was concerned. He'd been accused of stealing answers in a class he was good at, and his team couldn't beat Hobbs.

Lovington's JV also lost to Slaton (Texas) High School but rebounded with wins over Carlsbad, El Paso (Texas) Parkland, and Tucumcari high schools.

Their record was 6–2. But their final two games were against very talented teams: Portales and Artesia.

Portales had won a state title in 1988, and they had a stud defensive end who had dozens of sacks. Artesia's varsity was the defending state champion, and they had an unstoppable receiver being recruited by New Mexico State.

The receiver's name was David Patterson, and he'd had one of the most dominant games in state history against Hobbs earlier in the season. Patterson had seven touchdown catches and 329 receiving yards—the third-most ever in a single game!

With only two games left, Brian figured his team had nothing to lose. He pulled Stevie aside before the game against Portales.

"That d-end is going to be in your face all day long," Brian told Stevie. "Don't let him sack you. When you're in trouble, just throw the ball in my direction."

Stevie and Brian didn't know the defensive end's name—just that he wore No. 96. And No. 96 got to Stevie in a hurry on every single play.

Stevie did as Brian suggested, throwing the ball to his top

receiver whenever No. 96 was barreling toward him. For a while, the strategy worked because Brian was actually bigger, stronger, and could jump higher than the cornerback and safety defending him.

On defense, Brian was everywhere, making key tackles and knocking away a few passes.

It was a low-scoring game, and the two teams were tied at 14 with just two minutes left. With no timeouts remaining, Brian's team couldn't afford to hand the ball off to Ricky, so the game was in Stevie's hands.

"Let's go, Lovington!" Brian's mother screamed. "This is Wildcat Country!"

On the very next play, though, Stevie dropped back and reared back to throw the ball as No. 96 approached him. But when Stevie released the ball, No. 96 jumped straight up in the air and barely tipped the pass with his right pinky finger.

"No!" Stevie said, as the ball floated up high into the air.

Now it was a battle to see who would come down with it.

Stevie tried to slide underneath it, but he got drilled by another defensive lineman. No. 96 collected the ball with his two hands and sprinted toward the end zone. He didn't have any sacks, but he had the game-changing play—a 63-yard interception return for a touchdown.

Lovington got the ball back, and Brian caught four consecutive passes. But with two seconds left, Brian's team was still 45 yards from a touchdown to give them a chance to tie the game.

Stevie could hurl the football a long way, but would he have enough time to heave it toward the end zone? From the shotgun formation, Stevie got the snap, and he waited and waited.

One Mississippi, two Mississippi, he silently counted. Brian was sprinting along the left sideline. Before he could even think *three Mississippi,* Stevie was drilled by No. 96.

The game was over; Portales had defeated Lovington, 21-14.

Brian was very disappointed. He had worked really hard on defense and offense. He looked at Stevie, who walked with his shoulders slumped. Stevie's white jersey was caked in dirt and streaked with grass stains. Brian knew Stevie had done his best. He walked over to Stevie and patted him on his left shoulder.

"We almost had 'em," Brian said. "You played your heart out."

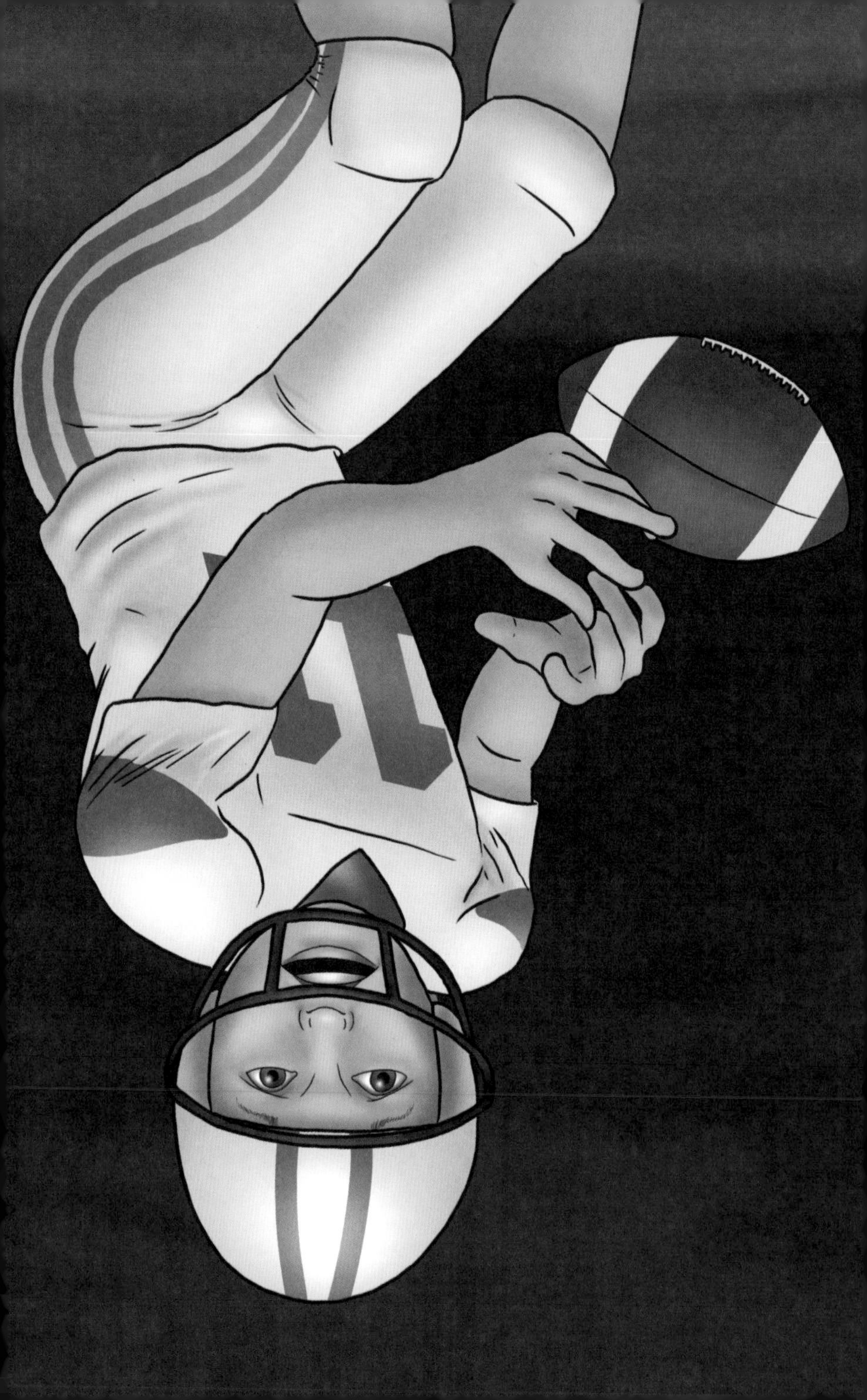

Chapter 18

The Wildcats Face a Powerhouse Program

The final game of the season was against Artesia, about an hour west of Lovington. Artesia had more football titles than any other school in the state. The Bulldogs' junior varsity and varsity teams were undefeated entering the game. In fact, both teams scored a lot of points and surrendered very few.

For Artesia's JV team, their closest game was 34–13.

"This is it," Coach Bryant told his players. "We're 6–3, and we have a chance to beat the Bulldogs. Do you guys believe you can do it?"

Brian certainly did. The Bulldogs were good, but Brian wasn't intimidated. All season he had shined on offense and defense—his confidence growing with each game.

Artesia opened with the ball, and Brian drilled the running back for a two-yard loss. On the next play, Brian blitzed, meaning he sprinted toward the quarterback when the ball was snapped. Brian didn't get the sack, but he forced the quarterback to throw a bad pass.

Brian was making his presence felt.

He was equally determined on offense, catching short passes and carrying defenders three or four extra yards before he collapsed to the ground due to exhaustion.

Brian inspired his teammates, who were also playing hard.

The two teams went back and forth, racking up the points. They were tied at halftime, 24–24, and they were tied after three quarters, 31–31. With four minutes to go, Artesia had a third-and-goal from Lovington's two-yard line. Artesia's massive offensive line tried to force their way into the end zone. They needed to create enough space for their backup running back to score. Brian slipped between two of the offensive linemen and stuffed the running back at the line of scrimmage for no gain.

"That's my boy!" Brian's mom yelled from the stands.

Artesia settled for the short field goal to take a 34–31 lead.

Lovington now had the ball, with a chance to win the game.

Stevie had one of his best games of the season, making a lot of important passes against Artesia's dominant defense. Five different Wildcats had at least one catch, so Stevie was keeping Artesia guessing. After a couple of completions, Lovington was near midfield, facing a second down. Brian ran a slant route, which means he started near the right sideline and headed at an angle toward the middle of the field. The cornerback chasing him tripped after about 10 yards, and Brian was wide open. As Stevie prepared to pass the ball, Brian peeked up the field, seeing no one between himself and the end zone.

Catch it and score, and Lovington would upset mighty Artesia. Brian's teammates would probably carry him off the field on their shoulders.

But as the ball touched his fingers, Brian quickly turned and looked up the field...only to have the ball slip through his grasp and onto the turf. It was an incomplete pass.

Even worse, Brian had literally dropped the ball.

He felt terrible for not finishing the play that he'd practiced so many times. He'd gotten distracted. He realized he had shifted his focus from catching and securing the ball to scanning the field and thinking about the game-winning play instead.

On third down, Stevie tried to complete a long pass to the team's starting tight end, but they couldn't make the play. Then on fourth down, Brian caught the pass on the far sideline, but he was stopped two yards short of the first-down marker.

The game—and Lovington's season—was over.

Brian was disappointed. Coach Faith waited for him on the sideline.

"Great game, Urlacher," Coach Faith said. "Keep your head up. See you in the spring."

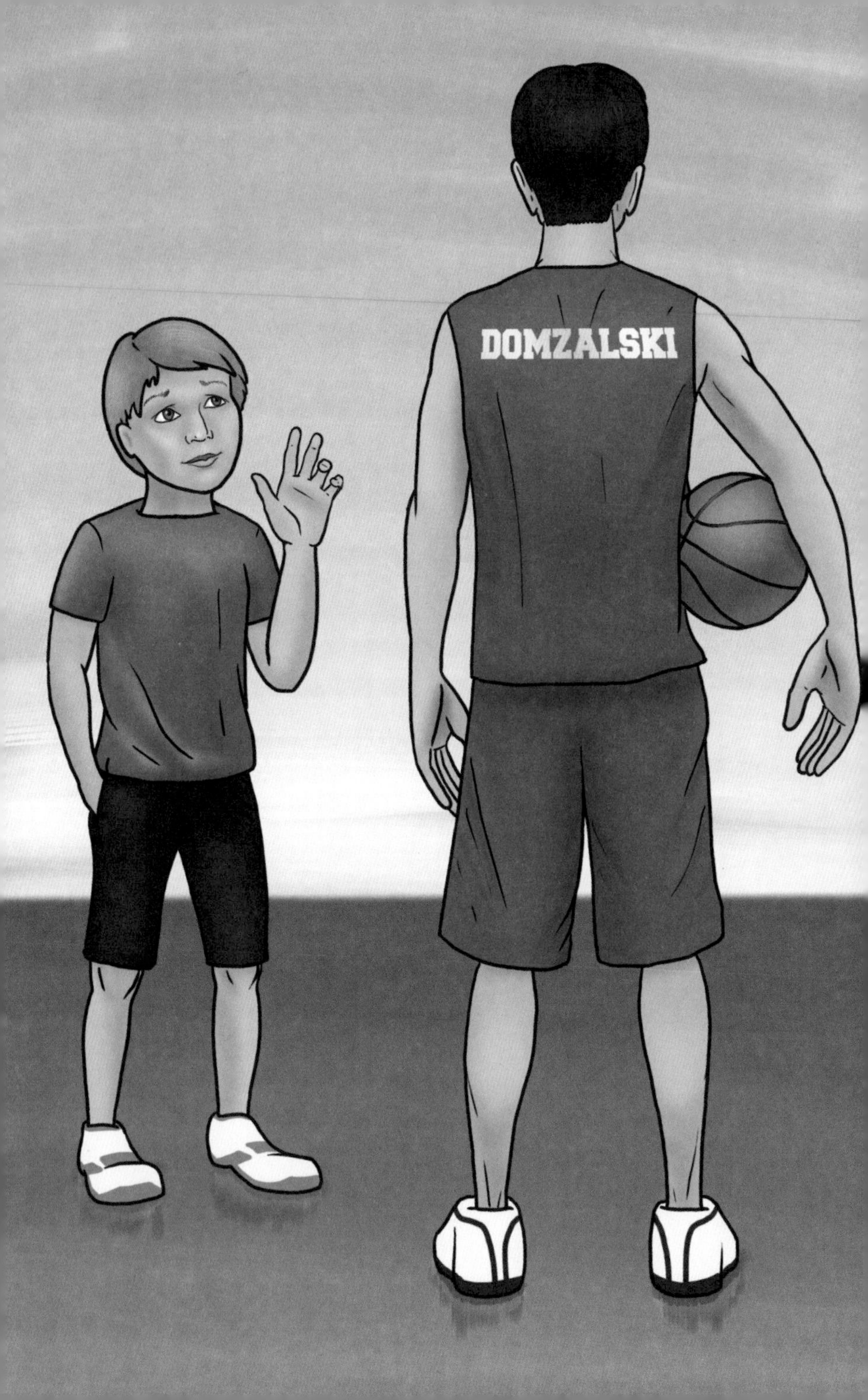
DOMZALSKI

Chapter 19

Seeing Stardom

Brian didn't have time to feel too bad. He had to jump right into basketball, which meant he'd get to spend more time with his best friend Brandon.

Since Brandon wasn't playing football, he had more time to practice dribbling, shooting, and playing defense. Brandon also spent a lot of time with his uncle Chief Bridgforth—the varsity basketball coach.

There was a lot of excitement about Lovington's basketball team because it had a legitimate star: one of the biggest in state history. His name was Taymon Domzalski.

His mother Joanne owned Nowell Prescription, the pharmacy in Lovington, and his father was a teacher and coach. Mr. Domzalski had actually played basketball at Western New Mexico University in Silver City.

Taymon was a gifted athlete who could do it all. He had something very few kids in Lovington possessed: natural size. Taymon was big—really big! Not a surprise since his father was 6 feet 6 inches, and his mother was 5 feet 9 inches. Taymon was 6 feet 5 inches in seventh grade.

Brian sometimes wondered what it would be like to be so tall *and* athletic.

That would be so cool, Brian thought. But he wasn't too envious.

Taymon was 6 feet 7 inches as a high school sophomore when he started to draw national attention from college coaches. Famous coaches like Bobby Knight of Indiana, Roy Williams of Kansas, Mike Krzyzewski of Duke, and Jim Harrick of UCLA visited tiny Lovington to check out Taymon in person.

And they weren't disappointed.

Sometimes big high school players play soft in the paint, but Taymon was aggressive on defense and offense. He was also unique because of his ability to run the floor and to shoot from outside.

Lovington's gym was always buzzing, with Chief constantly on the go because some major college coach always seemed to be in town to check out Taymon.

Taymon's parents, though, were very strict, expecting Taymon and his little sister to excel in academics. When it was the weekend, Taymon was never out and about hanging out with friends. He spent his free time studying or helping his parents.

All that, though, just made Taymon even more attractive to the big-time college coaches!

Lovington's JV and varsity teams didn't disappoint, getting out to strong starts. Taymon was the star, but several of his junior classmates were athletic and talented, and the Wildcats torched the competition.

On the JV team, Brian built on the momentum of his ninth

grade season. Although he wasn't big (just under 6 feet), Brian had long arms, and he could run and jump. In fact, after every practice, Brian would stick around and try to dunk the basketball. Brandon first grabbed the rim when he was in seventh grade, and Brian dunked a volleyball in ninth grade. Of their friends, Daniel was the first to dunk in practice—right at the end of their ninth grade season.

By 10th grade, Brian and Brandon could both dunk in practice, but they just couldn't do it in an actual game.

"I'll bet you a six-pack of Coke that I'll dunk in a game before you," Brandon told Brian.

"I'll take that!" Brian replied.

Other than from their parents, the JV players didn't get much attention, but they had a strong team with players who understood their roles. Brandon was selected to play on the varsity team. That meant Brian's role changed from grabbing rebounds and playing defense to shooting more.

The JV team was going to miss Brandon's 20-plus points per game.

"What are we gonna do without Brandon?" Daniel asked after the JV team lost consecutive games to Carlsbad and Artesia.

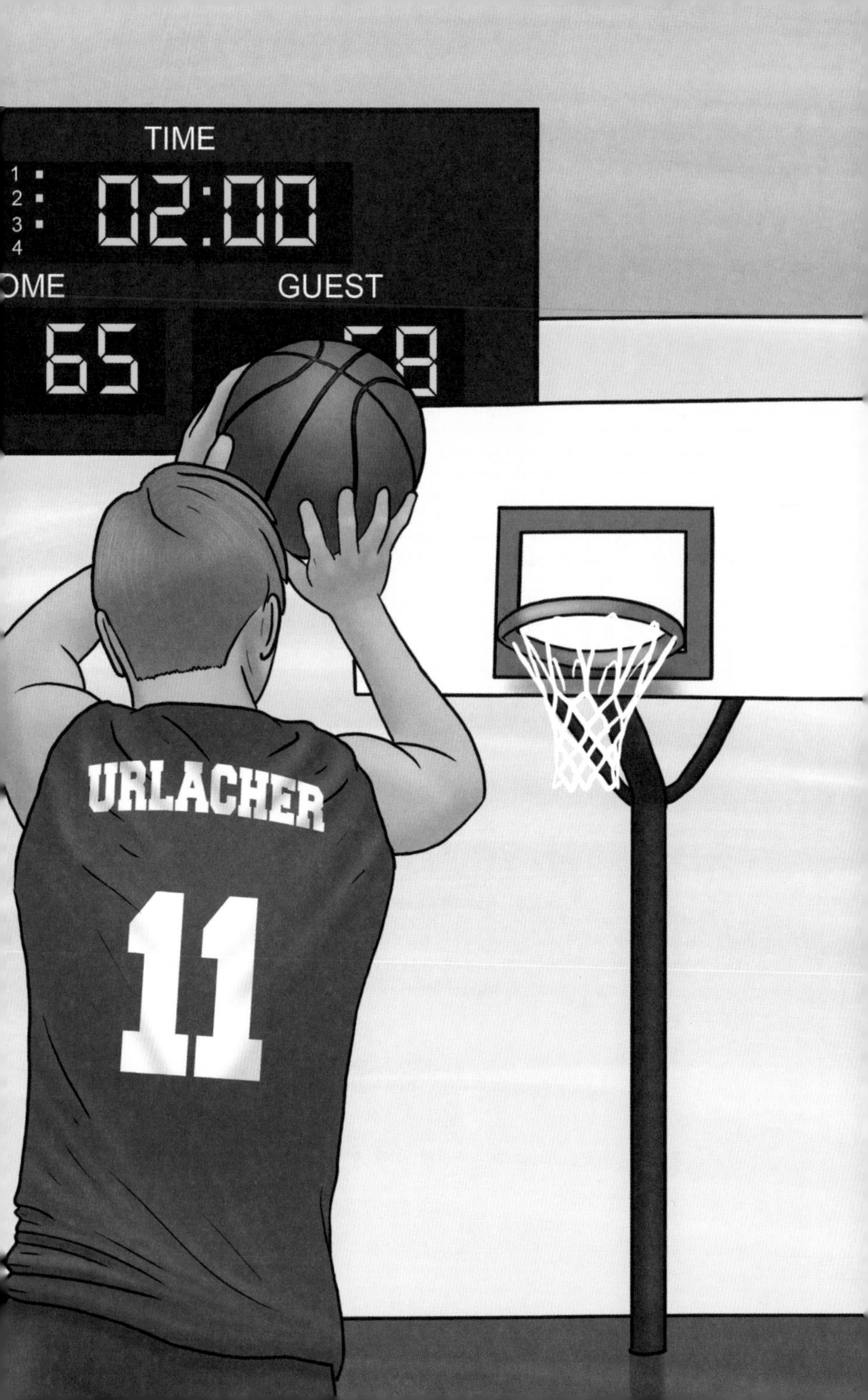
TIME
1
2
3
4
02:00
OME
GUEST
65
URLACHER
11

Chapter 20

Brian Has To Step Up in Basketball

Brian was happy that Brandon got the opportunity to suit up with the varsity team, but he didn't really play that much.

"If they're not going to use him," Brian told Daniel, "then they should let him play with us!"

Brandon was torn. He learned a lot by practicing with the varsity team, and he enjoyed being a part of such a talented team, but he missed playing in games, especially with his friends. Sometimes he wanted to say something, but he didn't want to disappoint his uncle, Chief Bridgforth.

Brian was averaging 10 points and 11 rebounds per game, but Lovington's JV team was struggling. Daniel challenged Brian to step up his game for the final two games against Eunice and Tucumcari.

"Brian, I know you can score more points," Daniel said. "We really need you to be more aggressive shooting the ball."

Brian had always focused on playing defense and grabbing

rebounds, but his team needed him to do more on offense.

Against Eunice, Brian attempted his first three three-pointers of the season, making two of them. He finished the game with a season-high 17 points, but Eunice held on for a 53-49 win.

"Great game!" Brian's mother told him afterwards.

But Brian wasn't the least bit happy.

"We lost, Mom," he said. "I didn't do enough."

In the JV team's final game of the season, they fell behind early to Tucumcari. The rim was being unkind to Brian and Daniel, who were missing shots they normally made. As they headed onto the court after halftime, down 38–30, Brandon intercepted Brian and Daniel.

"What's up, guys?" he said. "Are you gonna take these guys down for me?"

Brian and Daniel missed their first few shots of the second half, but their teammates kept the team in the game. Then, early in the fourth quarter, Brian and Daniel both started to get hot.

Their defense was starting to wear on Tucumcari, and Lovington was getting some easy fast-break points. With two minutes to go, they tied the game on Brian's three-pointer from the top of the key.

As soon as the ball splashed through the net, Brian recognized his mom's piercing shriek. When Tucumcari called a timeout, Brian couldn't help laugh as he headed toward the bench.

Heading back onto the court, Brian and Daniel high-fived, knowing they had all the momentum. Lovington scored 10 of the game's final 12 points, clinching the win.

Brian and Daniel finished with 20 points each.

"Great job," Brandon told Brian as the JV players walked off the court and the varsity players headed toward the bench before stretching.

"Go get 'em," Brian told his best friend.

Led by Taymon, Lovington's varsity team finished the regular season strong. But in the state semifinal game against Aztec High School, Lovington struggled with its shooting and was ousted.

Brian was disappointed for the varsity players, but he was excited about the next season. For the first time ever, he'd get to play with Taymon. Brian was curious to see how his game would stack up against Taymon, who was definitely going to be getting a scholarship to play basketball in a major college program.

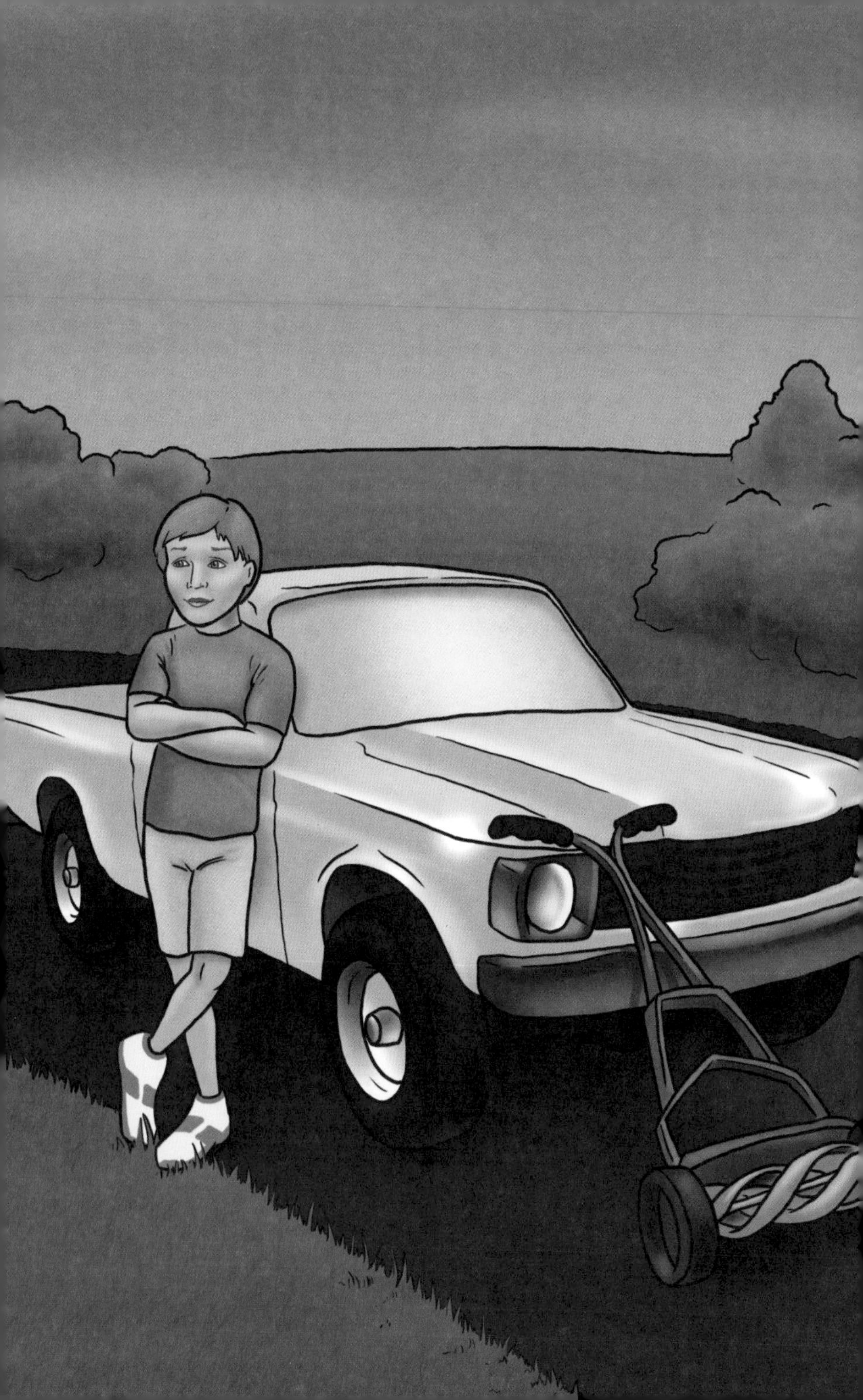

Chapter 21

Summer Shape

The summer before his junior year, Brian continued to show up consistently for Coach Q's early-morning workouts. Brian's birthday was May 25, and he had saved up $400 to buy his first car.

It was a Chevy LUV—an acronym for Light Utility Vehicle—but it was actually a modest truck without any fancy features. It was a four-speed, which represented the number of gears, and it was white.

Brian named his LUV *Stacy*.

The truck was more than 10 years old, and the passenger side door was tricky to open and close, but Brian and Casey loved that truck because they didn't need to rely on Troy to take them to school anymore for Coach Q's 5 a.m. workouts.

They had freedom!

The school was about a 10-minute drive from their house. After they finished their early workout, they would leave Stacy in a parking spot nearest the door they exited after school. Coach

Q would then drive them to his house, which was just a few blocks away, feed the boys, and let them shower up before school started.

Coach Q and his wife didn't have any children, and they liked having Brian and Casey over at the house. But the boys added a lot of money to their grocery bill because they would munch through boxes of Fruit Loops® and Trix®. They'd polish off a box of cereal and a gallon of milk every two days!

"Thanks Mrs. Q," Brian would say as he slurped the last of his bowl. "We'll see you tomorrow!"

The early-morning workouts were humbling for Brian. He was clearly the strongest player in his class, but there was a problem: his younger brother could out lift him in a couple of exercises.

Brian really *liked* to workout, but Casey *loved* to workout! Casey was, in many ways, better built for weight room success. He had shorter arms and legs, which meant he didn't have to push weights out as far from his body.

Coach Q recognized the rivalry between the two—and he enflamed it.

"Come on Brian! You gonna let your little brother squat 50 more pounds than you?" Coach Q would say. "You can't be serious!"

Brian was developing into a very good athlete. He had natural speed and moved very well. He was also very smart. But in terms of strength, Brian just couldn't seem to surpass Casey—and it really bothered him.

The football players usually did the same sets, cycling through different programs: chest and biceps on Monday, for instance, and quads and shoulders on Tuesday. To try and close the gap, Brian increased his daily goal of 100 pushups to 200 pushups, which he would do at nighttime. But when he did them, Casey would do them too.

Their house, after all, wasn't very big.

As a sophomore, Casey was already inching closer to some of Lovington's all-time weightlifting records. He was squatting 450 pounds, about 55 pounds less than the record. Casey never said anything, but he aimed to break those school weightlifting records before his big brother graduated high school.

The previous year, Brian had a hard time convincing his teammates to show up to Coach Q's morning workouts. But before their first varsity season, Brian's classmates started showing up regularly with him. Because he'd been training with Coach Q so long, Brian became one of the workout leaders, helping direct teammates in technique and the sequence of exercises.

When his sophomore year ended in the middle of June, Brian continued the morning workouts but then ramped up his mowing business. Just paying for the car wasn't enough. He also had to make money to pay for gas, insurance, and all the snacks and meals he wanted to make his summer special.

With his truck, Brian could take his operation beyond his neighborhood. He had his regular customers, and he added new ones through word-of-mouth referrals. His best customer was

still Mrs. Bradley. She was very active in the community and had lots of friends. She would tell all of them how great Brian was at tending to her lawn.

"Cheryl, you wouldn't believe how professional Brian is," Mrs. Bradley told one of her friends. "He always shows up on time, never asks for anything, and makes such straight lines."

Brian would sheepishly smile, but he was proud of his reputation.

In his spare time, Brian practiced football, playing catch with whoever was available. He sometimes did individual drills, working on his quickness and explosiveness. He was very excited about his first year of varsity football.

One evening, Casey and Sheri were both staying over at their friends' houses. Brian was sitting on the couch watching television when his mother initiated a conversation.

"How are you, Brian?" she asked.

"I'm doing great," Brian said.

"Is basketball still your favorite sport?" Brian's mother asked.

"Not anymore," Brian replied. "I'm gonna be a football player. I'm going to play for the Dallas Cowboys someday."

Brian's mother was stunned by his answer. Basketball had always been Brian's favorite sport. He wanted to play in the National Football League? She thought about the danger. She thought about the struggle. And she thought about the slim chance of him playing pro football.

Though a small town, Lovington had a proud football history, winning 11 state titles. In the 1960s, Wildcat teammates John Carrell and Leo Lowery both played at Texas Tech and were late-round picks in the 1965 NFL Draft.

Brian was a good player, but he wasn't even the undisputed star of his team.

Brian's mother, though, didn't want to crush his dream.

"If you're willing to put in the work," she said cheerily, "anything is possible."

Two days later at the grocery store, Brian's mother ran into Coach Faith. Anxious about her heart-to-heart conversation with Brian, she wanted to get some insight from Coach Faith. Never shy, she asked him what Brian's role would be for the upcoming season.

"Well, I expect that he'll get one of the starting receiver spots," Coach Faith said, "but I'm not sure where he'll fit in on the defense. We've got a lot of good players coming back."

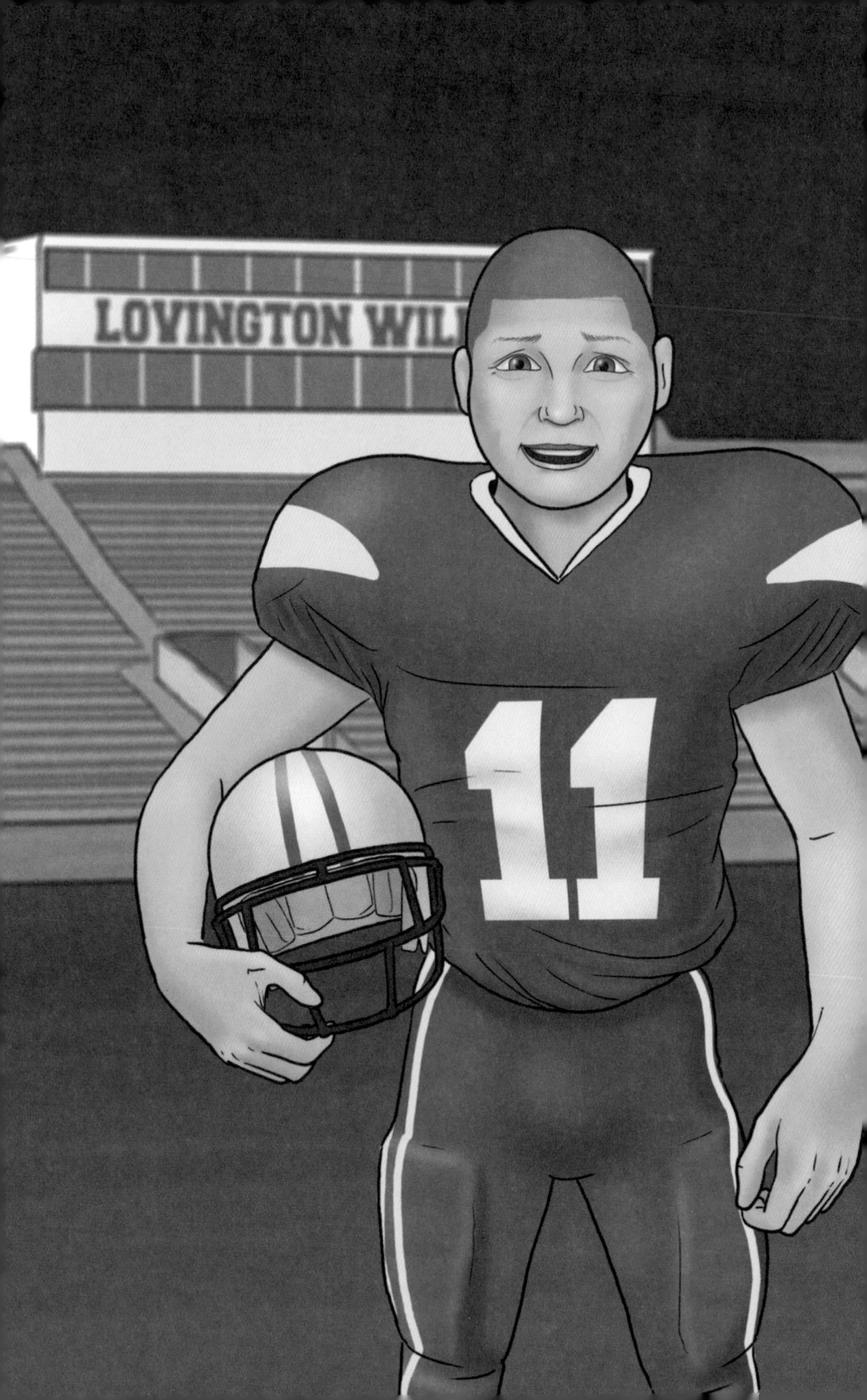
LOVINGTON WIL
11

Brian Breaks Out

In 1992, Coach Faith's second season as the head coach at Lovington, the Wildcats went 5-5. But in 1993, Coach Faith led the team to a 9-2 record and into the second round of the playoffs.

Expectations were high for the 1994 Wildcats.

Before two-a-days, Brian checked his height and weight. He was ecstatic! He was just under 6 feet 2 inches, and he weighed 185 pounds. In about a year, he'd grown three inches and added 20 pounds—nearly all of it muscle.

He was what coaches called "explosive." He'd always been a good leaper, but by working on his footwork, Brian also developed a quick first step.

Coach Faith needed a few offensive starters, but he returned all of his starting defensive players. During the 1993 season, the Wildcats allowed an average of 13 points per game.

Brian worked with the starting offense as a receiver and he played on special teams, but he was a backup safety on defense. He didn't care. He was excited to play in Wildcat Stadium in front of the whole town!

His first varsity game was against Eunice: a familiar opponent. Brian's junior varsity team played Eunice in the season opener the previous season and defeated them 30–13.

As usual, Brian's mom was at the game. Because it was his first varsity appearance, Troy, Sheri, and Casey also showed up. He wanted to make them all proud.

It didn't take long for Brian to make an impact. On Lovington's first offensive series, Brian ran a simple slant pass for 12 yards.

"First down! First down!" Brian's mom screamed.

She proved a point Brian had long suspected: even in a stadium, her voice rose above all others. Wildcat Stadium seated 5,500 fans, but Brian's mother made sure her son could hear her shouts of support, and he could see his step-dad vigorously applauding.

The Wildcats cruised to victory, 35–8, and Brian finished with six catches for 76 yards. He didn't score a touchdown, but he definitely contributed in his first varsity start.

The Wildcats' second game was against Deming, about five

hours west of Lovington. In the second quarter, Brian caught a short screen pass, stiff-armed the opposing cornerback, and ran 38 yards into the end zone. It was his first varsity touchdown!

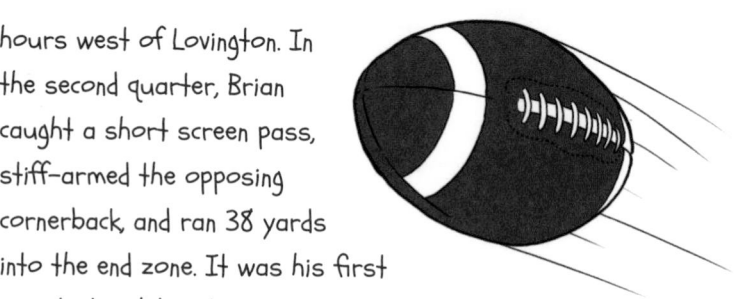

He scored his second on the next series, when he outleaped a defender in the end zone for a nine-yard touchdown.

But Brian got a surprise early in the fourth quarter, with Lovington up 42–7. Coach Faith called on Brian to enter the game as a safety. He was a little nervous because he had been working really hard to understand the offensive playbook, but Brian didn't waste any time making an impact on defense.

On the third play, Brian punched the ball out of a receiver's grasp, causing a fumble that one of his teammates recovered. On his eighth defensive snap, Brian batted away a pass intended for the tight end.

Brian felt very comfortable playing defense. He had a knack for knowing what the other team was trying to do and reacting very quickly. He was also a reliable tackler.

The Wildcats destroyed Deming 49–7.

The next day, Brian was called into Coach Faith's office.

"Urlacher, you're my new starting strong safety," Coach Faith told him. "I like the way you play defense. You're a natural."

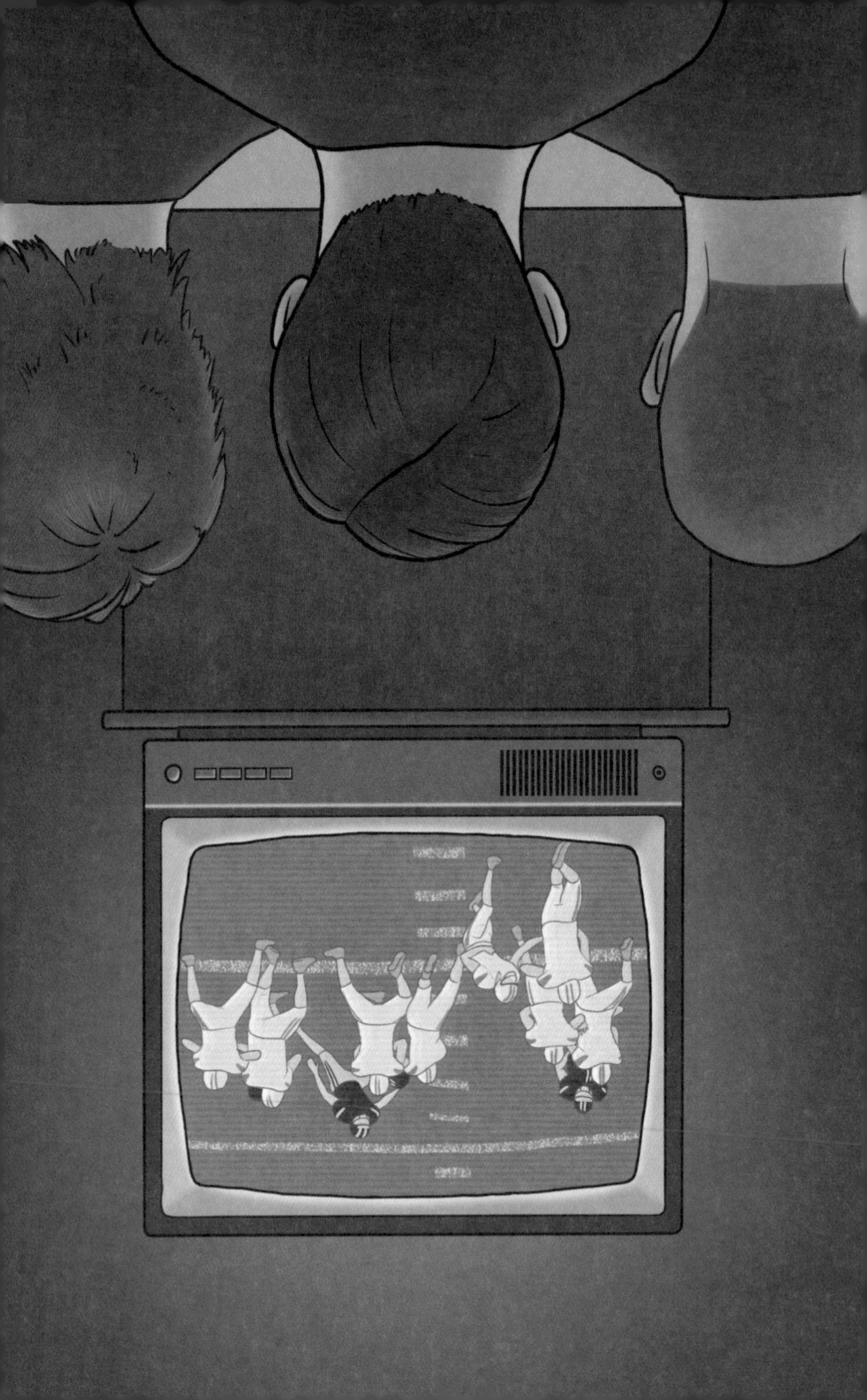

Chapter 23

No Cheap Shots

Brian couldn't have been any happier.

He was starting on offense and defense as a junior, and the Wildcats were rolling. They won their next three games by a combined score of 110–33, and Brian was making a name for himself with big plays. Against Hobbs, Brian even returned his first kickoff for a touchdown. He fielded the ball at the five-yard line and zigzagged down the field for a 95-yard touchdown.

But the Wildcats got into an offensive shootout in El Paso, Texas. Neither defense could stop the other team's offense. Lovington took the lead, 36–34, with just under two minutes left. But the Parkland Matadors had a secret weapon: a German exchange student who was a star soccer player.

That exchange student was Parkland's kicker, and he could make field goals from really far away. In the pre-game warm ups, Brian noticed him near midfield practicing super-long kicks.

The Wildcats knew they couldn't give him a chance to steal the game.

With 22 seconds left, the Matadors were a long ways from field-goal range. But one of Lovington's cornerbacks fell down near the sideline, and a Matador receiver raced down the field until Brian pushed him out.

With three seconds left, the Matadors lined up for a long field goal.

When the ball was snapped, Brian dove for the ball and nearly tipped it, but the line-drive kick went untouched toward the uprights. The ball was just long enough for a 52-yard field goal. Parkland's players jumped for joy, celebrating a 37–36 win.

When the teams lined up afterwards, Brian noticed a few of Parkland's players refused to shake his hand. He didn't know why. All Brian knew was that the Wildcats' hopes of an undefeated season were dashed.

Brian was sad about the loss, but he was even sadder the next morning.

The day after every game, the team gathered to watch film. Coach Faith controlled the remote, and he'd point out the highs and lows of their performance. In the second quarter, Parkland's running back was tackled to the ground by a defensive end and linebacker. A split second later, Brian dove into the pile and hit Parkland's player in the back.

"Ouch," a few of Brian's teammates quietly said, wincing at the replay.

On the opening kickoff of the second half, Brian drilled Parkland's returner late, after he'd run out of bounds. Then, late in the third quarter, Brian jumped on top of a pile after the play had been whistled dead.

Coach Faith lit into Brian.

"You need to grow up, Urlacher!" the Coach screamed. "That's garbage."

Brian was embarrassed. He loved scoring touchdowns. Other teams tried to neutralize Brian as a receiver, even assigning two defenders to cover him. But there wasn't anything anybody could do to slow him down on defense.

He loved drawing the "ooohs" and "ahhs" from fans after a big tackle, and he liked to make the opposing receivers think he was going to drill them even if he wasn't anywhere near them.

Brian figured he was fine if he didn't get flagged, but Coach Faith made it clear that wasn't the point.

Before the next game at Wildcat Stadium, Brian looked at the words posted in their locker room: *Work hard... Do what's right.*

Brian realized he needed to do a better job of playing until the whistle—but not a second after it. In the end, he wanted to be a good leader not just a good player.

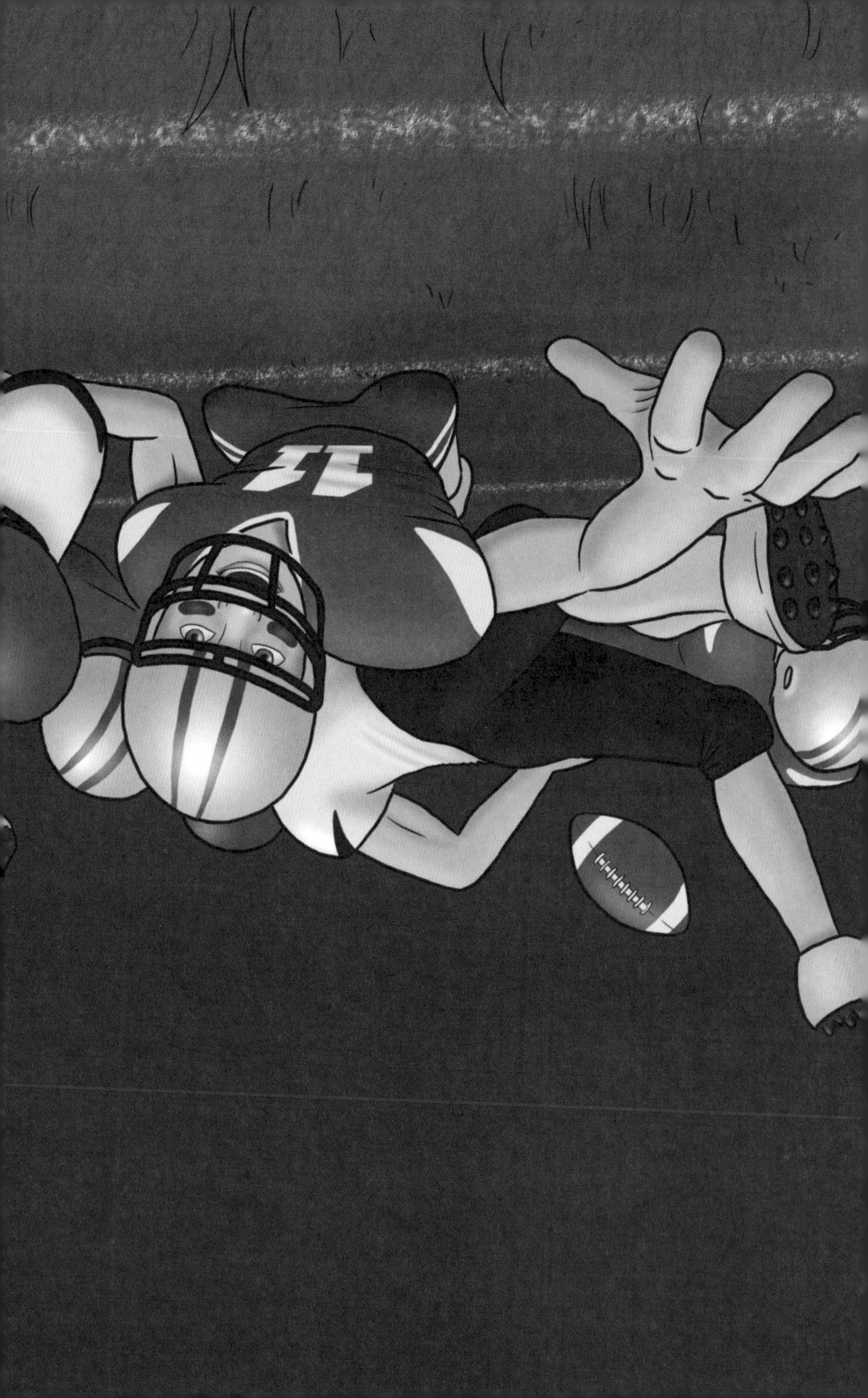

Chapter 24

The Injury

Two weeks later, the Wildcats lost to powerhouse Artesia, 27–11. They rebounded against Tucumcari, winning 36–15. Then they had a game against Portales. Lovington had won five consecutive games against Portales, but several of the games were really close. The Wildcats knew not to overlook the Rams.

On the opening kickoff, Brian sprinted down the field and disappeared into a mass of players. Bodies fell all over as the Rams' returner crumpled to the ground. Six players were stuck in a pile, and one of the Rams fell backward—right onto Brian's wrist.

"Owwww!" Brian howled. He knew something was wrong. He immediately felt a sharp pain, and his left wrist went limp.

Dr. Bob Smith rushed onto the field to take a look at Brian's wrist. Brian hoped to hear good news; he hadn't gotten hurt since he broke his right arm hopping a fence in third grade. Dr. Bob looked very serious.

"He's done for the night, Coach," Dr. Bob said. "He needs to go the emergency room."

Brian was afraid because his wrist started to swell up right away. When he got to the sideline, his mom was waiting for him.

She looked scared too. Brian's wrist was pointed at a funny angle.

"Mom, am I gonna be OK?" Brian asked.

"I don't know, Brian," she said. "We'll have to wait and see."

Brian's mom and step-dad drove Brian to the Children's Hospital in Lubbock, almost two hours away. They waited and waited, and Brian worried about what the doctor would tell him.

Will I miss the rest of the season? Do I need a big cast? he thought.

Brian had to get an x-ray—a technology that is so powerful it can take pictures of bone structure. After fifteen minutes, a nurse brought Dr. Williams a black sheet with blurry white blobs on it.

"Well, here's your x-ray, Brian," Dr. Williams said. "The good news is that all the bones are fine. But you have a dislocated wrist—that means your wrist isn't lined up properly. We'll have to reset it. And you have some ligament damage, so we have to protect it. We'll put a hard cast on it, and it'll heal up in a couple weeks."

"So I can't play football the rest of this season?" Brian asked.

"If everything heals," Dr. Williams said, "you could play in the postseason."

Brian was disappointed. But he couldn't feel sad for too long;

Dr. Williams still had to get his wrist pointed in the right direction.

"Now Brian, this is going to hurt," Dr. Williams warned. "But it won't hurt for very long, and your wrist will look normal again right away."

Dr. Williams grabbed Brian's left wrist with both of his hands, and he firmly twisted. Brian felt a little pain, but he didn't cry or complain.

"That wasn't so bad," Brian said.

As Brian and his parents were packing up, Dr. Williams mentioned one other thing.

"By the way," he said, "I took a closer look at the x-ray, and I think Brian will still grow three to four inches."

Brian was suddenly very excited.

"You hear that, Mom?" he said.

Brian had always been small. He never expected to grow much, and now he knew he was going to be big.

The next day, during practice, Brian and his mom visited with Coach Faith.

"He's going to be out a few weeks, Coach," Brian's mom said.

Coach Faith was disappointed because Brian was the team's third- or fourth-best option on offense, and he was becoming one of Lovington's top defenders.

"But guess what, Coach?" Brian said. "The doctor said I'm gonna grow another three or four inches before I graduate!"

For the first time ever, Coach Faith realized Brian Urlacher might have the potential to play in college.

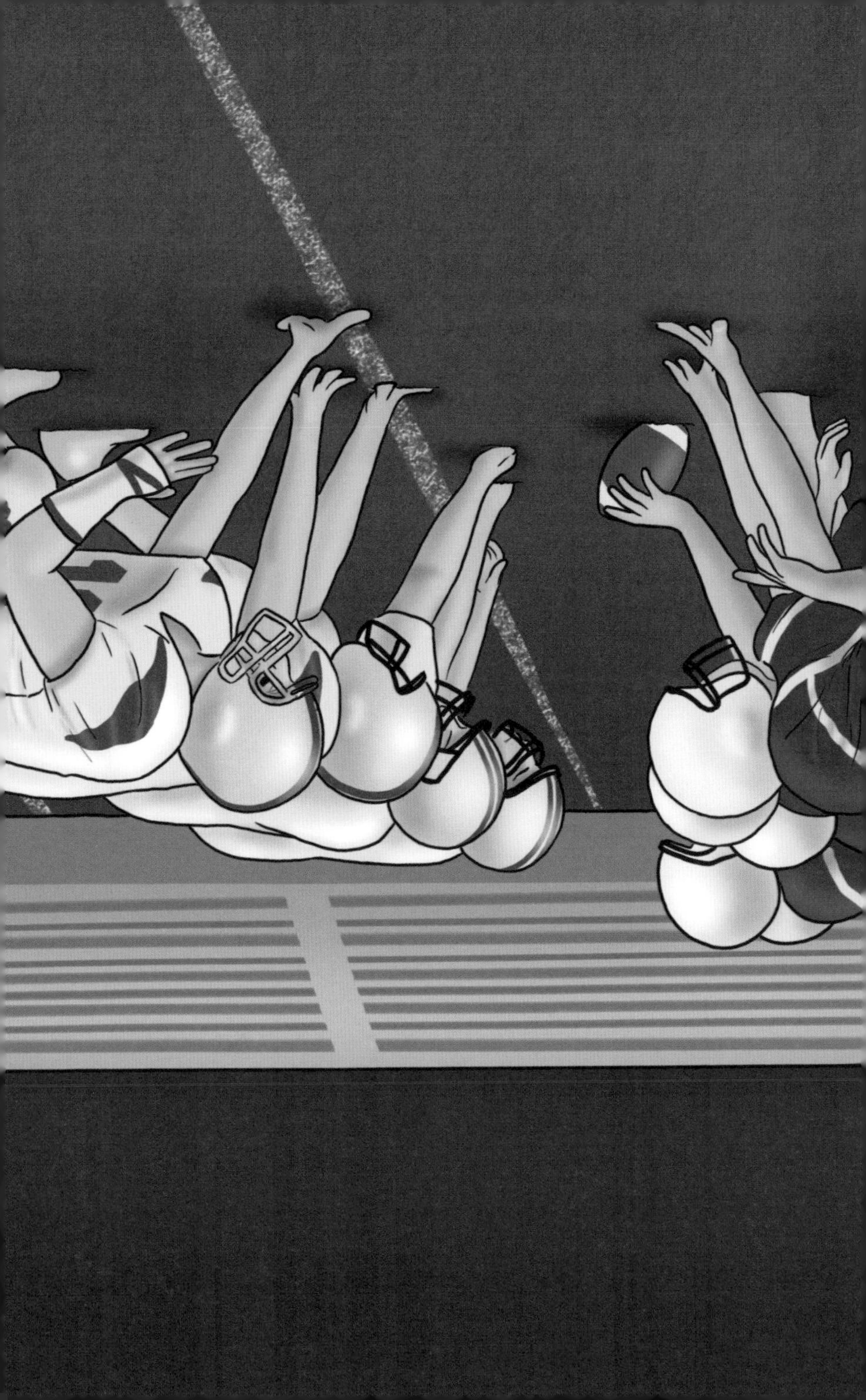

Chapter 25

Playing Through Pain

With Brian unable to finish the game, the Wildcats lost 28–24 to Portales. There was only one regular-season game left. Then all playoff teams had a week off before the first-round post-season games.

Brian sat on the bench, sporting his white cast with blue writing (representing the Wildcats' colors). Lovington trounced Tohachi 49–14 in the final regular season game.

After getting the approval of Dr. Williams, Brian readied himself to face Silver City. With his left hand in a cast, he knew he wouldn't be effective as a receiver. Brian, though, was willing to do whatever his coaches asked him to do.

They wanted him to focus on defense, so Brian helped Lovington keep the score low. In the fourth quarter, the game was tied 7–7.

Silver City had a lot of good defenders, so Coach Faith decided to call one of his trick plays—an end around. This is a running play when the receiver carries the ball around the end of his offensive line.

The players were puzzled by the call.

Brian had a cast on his left hand and the other starting receiver, Anson Brown, had a cast on his right hand. But the players did as they were told, and Brian took the handoff and ran toward the right side of his offensive line. When Silver City's fast defense shifted toward him, Anson drifted toward the left sideline.

Brian then tossed the ball across the field, with his right hand. Anson couldn't really catch the ball cleanly, so he tucked his elbows close to his side, and he waited for the ball to come.

Anson cradled the ball, turned, and ran down the field until he was tackled. The play earned the Wildcats 24 yards, setting up a game-winning field goal! They won 10–7.

The Wildcats cruised to a 33–0 win over Aztec High School, setting up a state title game against mighty Artesia. The Wildcats were a strong team, but the undefeated Bulldogs were bigger.

Lovington didn't back down from the Bulldogs, but the Wildcats slowly lost control of the game. They could score, but the Bulldogs' quarterback Paul Maupin was in a zone. Maupin connected on 25 of his 29 passes for 245 yards with four touchdowns and no interceptions.

By the end of the game, thanks to good blocking by his offensive linemen, Maupin's jersey looked as clean as when he put it on.

Lovington lost 35–21. The two teams lined up to shake hands. But one of Artesia's running backs, Jessie Cole, made a rude remark.

"Maybe next year, losers," Jessie said before he started to laugh.

Brian didn't say anything.

I'll show him, Brian thought.

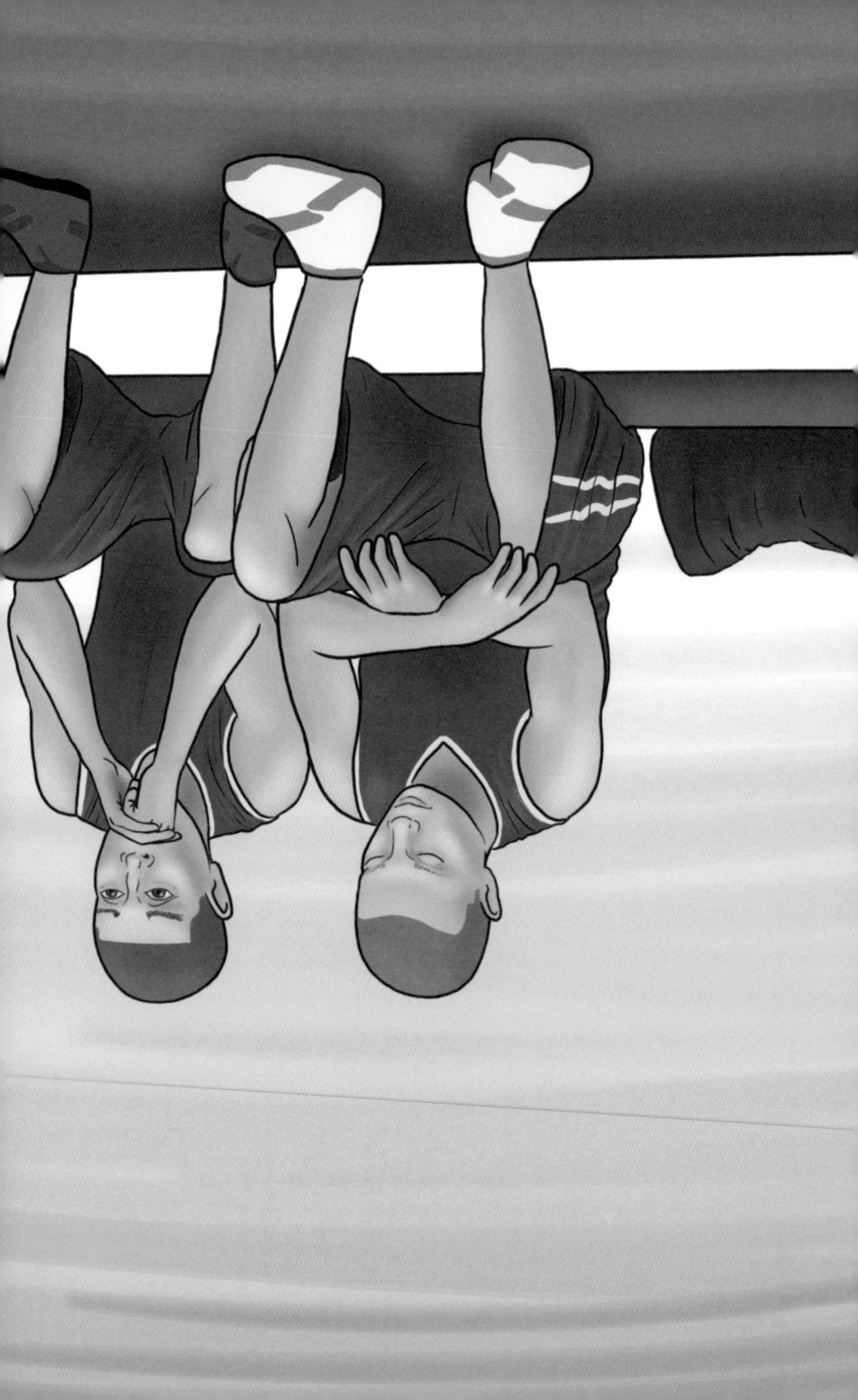

Chapter 26

Surprising Run

With football over, Brian shifted his focus to basketball. But before the basketball season started, the players discovered big news: Taymon wasn't going to play at Lovington anymore. It wasn't entirely clear why. Taymon transferred to New Mexico Military Institute in Roswell, New Mexico.

For years and years, Brian had looked forward to playing with Taymon, but he wouldn't get the chance. Although the Wildcats had a good team, Taymon would have made them one of the favorites to win a state title.

"Oh well," Brian said to Brandon, "we'll just win the state title without him."

With Taymon out of the picture, Brandon was once again his team's best player—but Brian was quickly closing the gap. He was a full 6 feet 3 inches, and he weighed nearly 200 pounds. He was still an explosive jumper who grabbed a lot of rebounds. Brian was also emerging as a scoring option. He improved his shooting and his ability to make layups around the basket.

In fact, by season's end, he even dunked in a game, winning the six-pack-of-Coke bet with Brandon!

Brian and Brandon were still best friends. In a game against Silver City, Brandon got fouled hard when he was going in for a layup and slammed into the padded wall. The Silver City player got in Brandon's face. Brian rushed over and tossed the Silver City player about 10 feet away toward the free-throw line.

Although the Silver City instigated the skirmish, Lovington was assessed a technical foul: that gave Silver City two free throws and the ball! Brian had no regrets because he was defending his best friend.

Brian and Brandon didn't act like friends in practice though. When they defended each other, one of them would foul the other too hard—and they'd both end up running laps. Neither conceded a layup, even if they were beaten.

"Knock it off, you two!"

Chief Bridgforth would yell at them. "You're supposed to be teammates!"

The Wildcats barely had a winning record, and they needed to beat Portales to earn a spot in the postseason. The Wildcats fell behind early as both Brian and Brandon struggled with their shooting.

The two started bickering at each other, and Chief Bridgforth did something he'd never done: he benched *both* of them. Lovington's two best players weren't on the floor as Portales extended its lead to 10...and then 14 points.

After a few minutes—which felt like hours to the boys who rarely sat out—Chief came to the end of the bench. He looked at Brian, he looked at Brandon, and then he leaned toward them.

"Are you two crybabies done yet?" he said.

Stunned, Brian and Brandon looked at each other.

"Because if you're done," Chief said, "we can still win this thing."

With just a few minutes until halftime, Brian and Brandon were both fired up, and they helped cut Portales' lead to eight points. Then, in the second half, Lovington took control late in the third quarter, and they cruised to a 75–63 win.

But the Wildcats didn't make it to the state tournament that season, losing to Artesia in the district tourney.

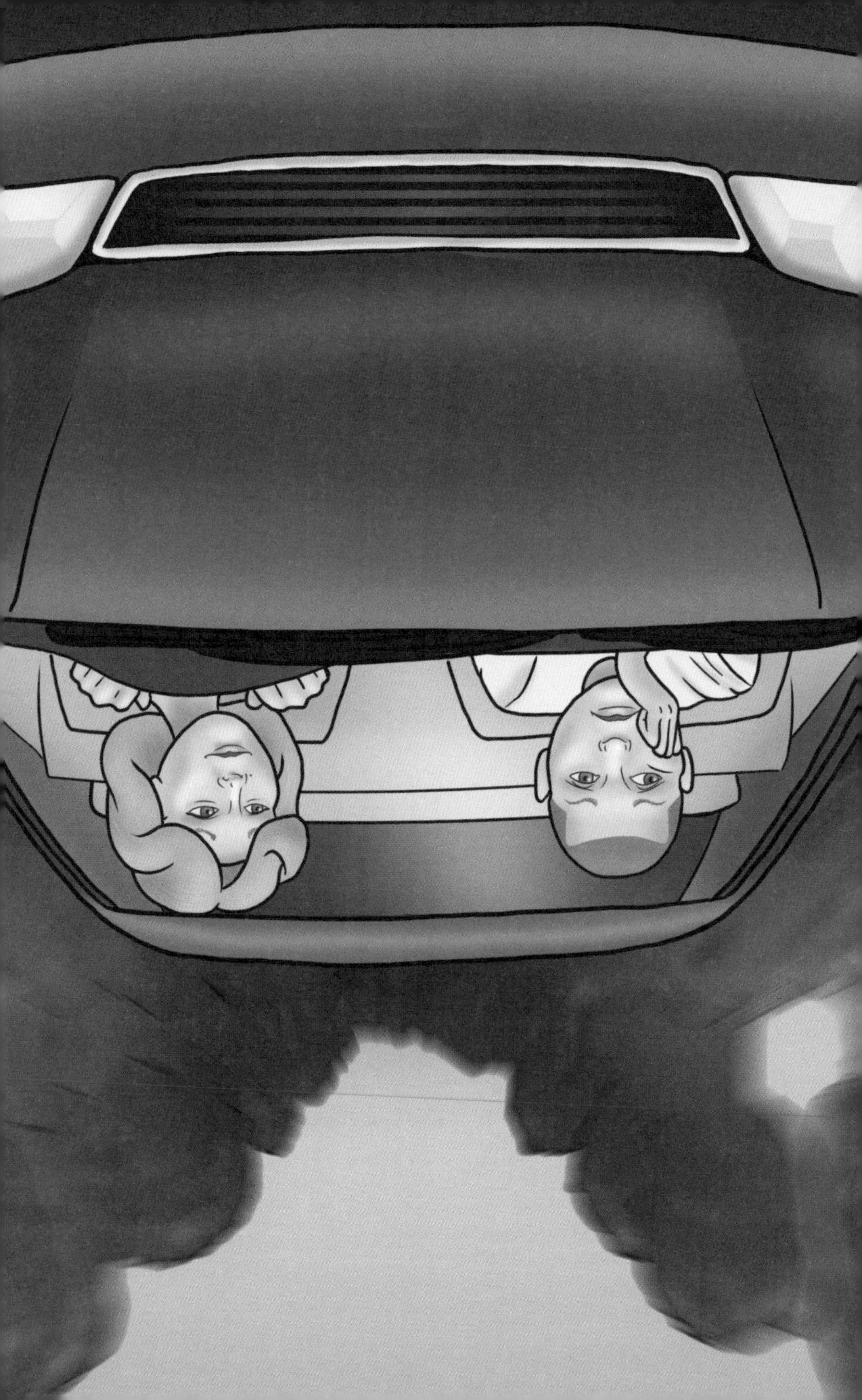

Chapter 27

Not Feeling the Love

Heading into the spring of his junior year, Brian started to think about his future. He had a good football season, but he wasn't getting much attention from colleges. Brian, of course, dreamed of playing at Texas Tech, but they hadn't shown any interest in him.

Brian got a few letters from Division II schools, offering him a chance to walk on. That meant they wouldn't grant him any scholarship money but would allow Brian to try out for the football team. That wasn't an option because Brian's family didn't have any money for college.

Sheri was the star of Lovington's girls' basketball team, and she was recruited by colleges during her sophomore year.

Brian figured he'd work in the oil fields after graduating, but he wanted to try his hardest during his senior year of football and basketball.

Brian and Casey continued their commitment to Coach Q's early morning workouts. It was really paying off for Brian because he was starting to get thicker and stronger. Brian was then 6 feet 4 inches and weighed 208 pounds.

By summertime, Casey was starting to break the records, just as he had aimed to.

As fall approached, Brian couldn't wait for the football season to start. He would get a chance to play with Casey as well as Brandon who had decided to play football again. The 1995 Lovington football team was going to be special.

Casey's JV team was very talented, featuring Chris Paloma. He was a dual-threat quarterback, which meant he could run and throw well. Chris was so skilled Texas Tech invited him to their summer football camp.

As Coach Faith registered Chris, though, he copied the form and signed Brian up too. Coach Faith was certain the Texas Tech coaches would be impressed with Brian who was going to be the Wildcats' star.

Brian was pumped when he arrived at Texas Tech's practice facility where there were several sparkling fields and bright-red blocking sleds. If the coaches didn't know who he was before the camp, Brian was sure they would know who he was afterwards. It was Red Raiders or bust for Brian!

During the all-day camp, Brian really concentrated to make sure he didn't make any mistakes. He even returned punts and kickoffs, showing off his versatility. But when the camp was over, nobody said a word to Brian.

Brian's mother eagerly waited in her car for an update on their long drive home from Lubbock.

"So how did it go?" she asked.

"I don't want to talk about it," Brian said.

Brian's mom could sense the disappointment in her son's voice.

They had a quiet two-hour drive back to Lovington on U.S. Route 82.

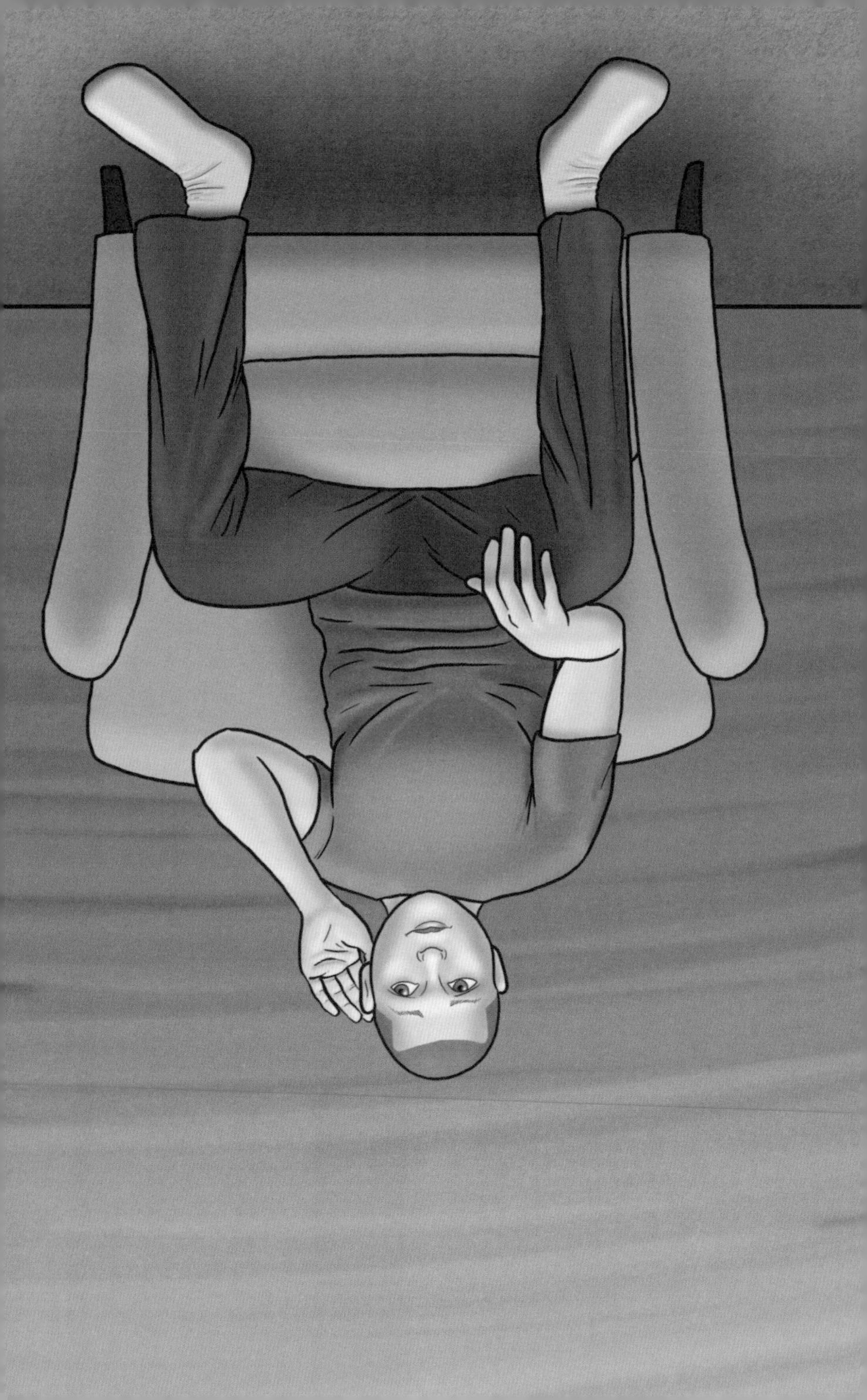

Chapter 28

Encouragement from Big Sis

Just before Brian's senior year, his sister Sheri had earned a basketball scholarship to New Mexico Junior College in nearby Hobbs. Sheri was the first in the family to go to college! Everyone was very proud of her.

One summer day, after mowing a few lawns, Brian came home and assumed nobody was around. After he quietly unlocked the door and walked inside, he realized Sheri was in her room on the telephone.

Brian plopped down on the couch in the living room, trying to enjoy some peace and quiet, but his sister was, as usual, talking loudly. It sounded like she was chatting with one of her new teammates.

The initial topics didn't interest Brian: the basketball team's practice schedule and the classes they were planning to take in

the fall. But then they talked about their families. Brian couldn't hear what Sheri's teammate was saying, but he could kind of piece together their conversation.

Sheri talked about how proud she was of Brian and Casey for doing the early morning workouts. Then Sheri talked about how excited she was about her brothers getting to play varsity football together.

"They're really competitive with each other," Brian heard Sheri say, "but they're going to be superstars for the Wildcats."

Now Brian was interested.

Sheri would *never* compliment him or Casey to their faces.

"What do you mean it doesn't matter?" Sheri said, clearly outraged. "No, Lovington isn't a big town, and we don't send football players to big schools. But you watch: Brian is going to be somebody."

After a reply, Sheri annoyingly responded, "No, I'm not crazy. You'll see."

Sheri slammed down the phone.

Brian was flattered by her comments and inspired by her faith in him. *Sheri got a college scholarship,* he thought, *so she must know what she's talking about.*

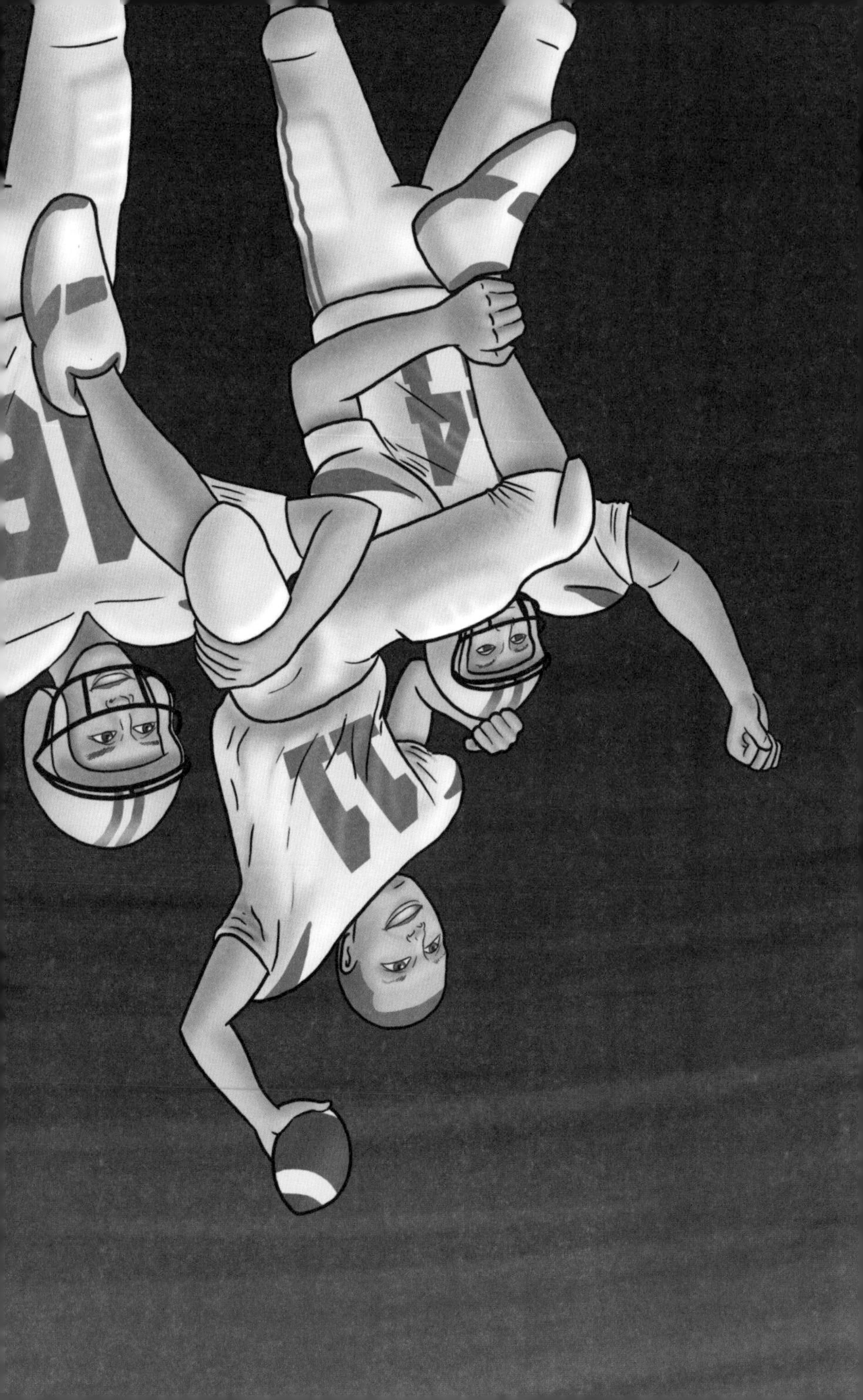

Chapter 29

Indispensable Brian

During games, Brian didn't come off the football field for the Wildcats. He was the team's No. 1 receiver and offensive option, the defense's best playmaker, and the kickoff and punt returner.

Lovington steamrolled their opponents to start the 1995 season.

They opened the season against Socorro: a town four hours west of Lovington. In the game, Brian returned a punt *and* a kickoff for touchdowns. He also had a receiving touchdown and some big tackles.

The Wildcats outscored Socorro, Deming, Hobbs, Santa Rosa, and Carlsbad 229–17 and earned a 5–0 record. That means the average score of each game was 45 for Lovington and a field goal for the opponent!

Brian, though, wasn't motivated to score as many touchdowns as he could. He wanted to be a good sport as an example for his younger teammates. When the Wildcats would get a big lead, he'd sidle up to Coach Faith and quietly ask him to let one of the backups get some playing time.

It was not hard to recognize Brian's importance to the Wildcats. But when reporters from the Lovington Leader or the Hobbs News-Sun—the two local newspapers—would ask to speak to him, Brian would politely decline.

The Wildcats had played together for a long time. Each player had grown so much from their middle school days when they couldn't even win a game. Brian didn't think it was fair for him to get so much of the credit.

Lovington was the No. 1 ranked team in the 3A football division. The team's first big challenge of the season, though, was against Roswell, the No. 3 ranked school in the bigger 4A division. The Coyotes played in the Wool Bowl—one of the most recognizable high school stadiums in the state.

Roswell had a powerful running back named Michael Gray. Michael wasn't fast, but the defense usually needed at least two players to wrestle him to the ground. On Roswell's first play, Michael took the handoff and ran to his left, between the center and guard. Just as he arrived at the line of scrimmage, Brian arrived too.

Smash!

Michael crumpled to the ground—and Brian didn't need any help. He made the tackle all by himself. Over and over again, Brian tackled Michael who grew tired late in the second quarter.

After four quarters, the game was tied 13–13.

In overtime, the Coyotes quarterback broke loose for a 38-yard run, and he completed a six-yard touchdown pass to his tight end. The Coyotes then led 20–13.

The Wildcats had to immediately answer with a touchdown or else they would lose.

Coach Faith highlighted Brian on the series, lining him up in the backfield and motioning him at different receiver spots. Chris was sharp, completing four consecutive passes to get his team into Roswell's red zone.

On third down, from Roswell's eight-yard line, Chris dumped the ball to his backup running back Eric Black. Eric avoided the first tackler and easily scored the touchdown.

All Lovington needed was an extra point to tie the game, but Coach Faith called "Carlsbad."

"What did he say?" Chris asked.

Carlsbad was a trick play from the extra point formation. Lovington was going for the win! Brian lined up on the right side, and Brandon lined up on the left side. When the ball was snapped, the holder pretended to put the ball down for the kicker. Brandon, instead of blocking, sprinted into the backfield. The holder tossed Brandon the ball, and he continued to run right. As the startled Roswell players closed in on Brandon, he squared up and stepped forward to make his throw.

I've got to make this work, Brandon thought.

The ball wobbled and floated through the air, and Brian was on the opposite side of the field waiting for it to arrive. Brandon didn't throw a spiral because he had a glove on. Yet, the ball landed in Brian's arms, and he stepped across the goal line for the two-point conversion.

Lovington won 22–21.

The Wildcats swarmed Brian in the end zone, and Brian's mother screamed nonstop for two minutes.

"Yeah, Brian! Yeah, Brian! Yeah, Brian!" she yelled over and over. Troy pumped his fist with excitement.

All of Lovington understood the significance of that win: the Wildcats might be in for an unforgettable season.

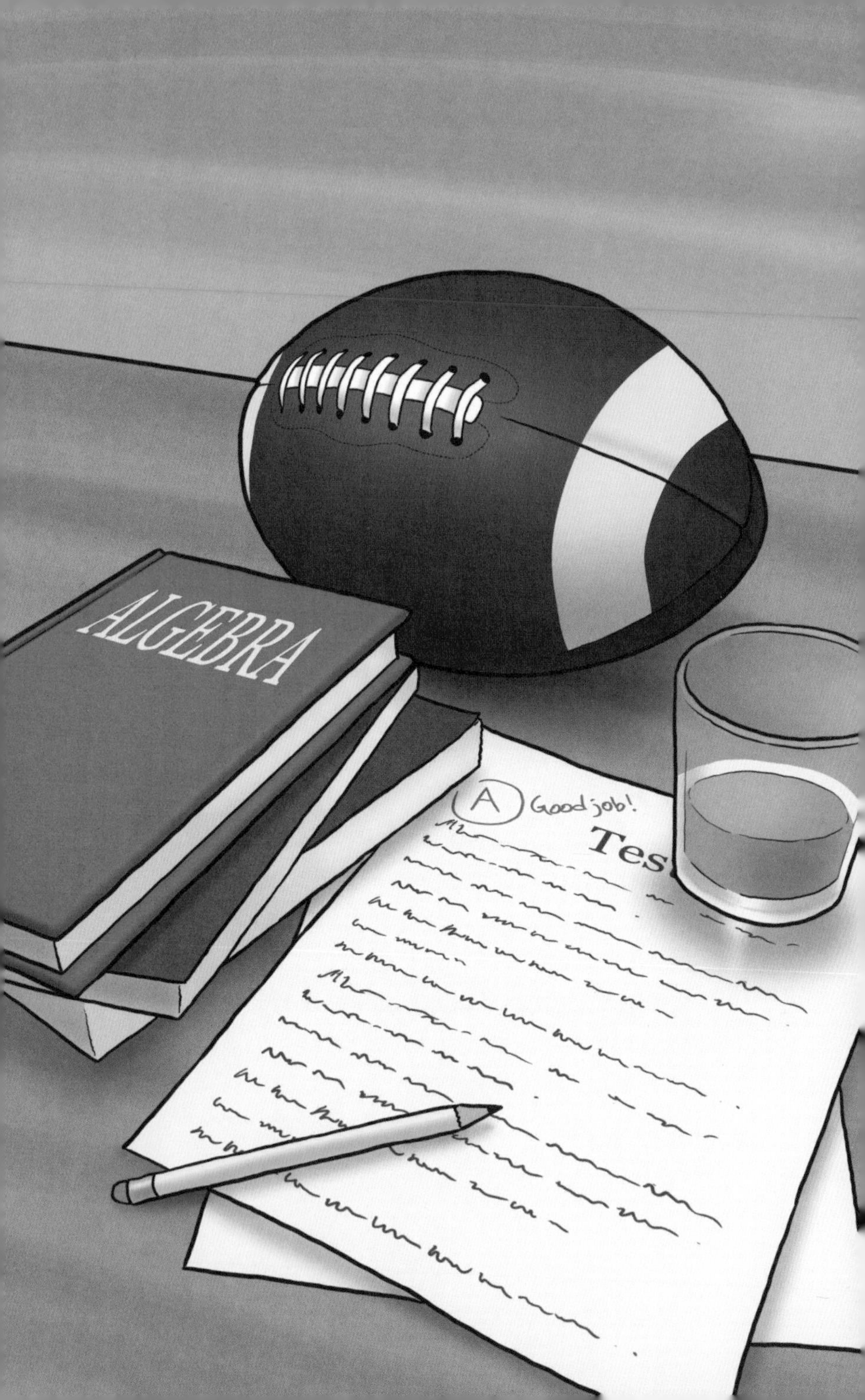
ALGEBRA
A
Good job!

Chapter 30

Putting It All Together

Lovington was a five-stoplight town, and there weren't many entertainment options for teenagers. For fun, Brian and Brandon would cruise up and down Main Street in Brian's Chevy LUV and drink chocolate milk.

Others would often flag them down to talk sports because Brian and Brandon were two of the most popular athletes in town. People in Lovington were proud of them because they were also good students, mostly earning As with an occasional B mixed in.

After two more wins, the Wildcats were 8–0 heading into their big game against Artesia. The Bulldogs had won three consecutive state titles and 18 overall. That was more than any other school in New Mexico! They had also won the last five games against the Wildcats, including in the state championship the previous year.

Coach Cooper Henderson, a legend in the state, led the Bulldogs. He was tough and demanding. Coach Henderson's players had short haircuts, wore ties on game day, and referred to all elders as sir or ma'am.

No exceptions.

Like Lovington, Artesia was undefeated, but they had allowed only 20 points all season! Quarterback Paul Maupin led the offense. He had played brilliantly against the Wildcats in the state championship game the previous year.

At least the game was at Wildcat Stadium.

The stands were packed, and hundreds of fans lined up on the track circling the field. It was considered the most important regular-season game for Lovington in a long time.

As the two teams stretched, Brian noticed Jessie Cole, the Bulldogs running back who had called them losers after the championship game. Brian knew he would need to be at his best—on offense, defense, and special teams—if the Wildcats were going to have a chance to win.

The Bulldogs got the opening kickoff, and the Wildcats wanted to make sure this game didn't start the way the last one finished. They needed to put some pressure on Maupin. Coach Faith and his coaches decided a conservative game plan against Maupin wouldn't work. They had tried that approach in the last championship game.

"We're going to have to blitz him,"

Coach Faith told his assistants in the planning meeting days before the game. "Relying on just our defensive line to pressure Paul isn't going to be enough."

A blitz is a high-risk, high-reward strategy for a defense.

Offenses typically have five offensive linemen blocking for the quarterback. A traditional defense calls for four defensive linemen to try and get to the quarterback on passing plays. A blitz requires one or more of the other defensive players—cornerbacks, linebackers, or safeties—to pursue the quarterback.

This can sometimes confuse a quarterback and his blockers. But blitzing means an opposing offensive player may not be covered. If the quarterback can identify the hole in the defense, then his offense can make a big play.

On the opening snap, as he dropped back, Maupin was flustered because Brian and a cornerback blitzed him. The Bulldogs weren't ready for a safety and a cornerback to come after Maupin, and Brian reached the quarterback first to register the sack.

The Wildcats' sideline erupted in cheers and high-fives.

On the next play, Casey, a defensive end, slipped past Artesia's offensive linemen and sacked Maupin. On third down, the Wildcats blitzed a linebacker, and Maupin completed a pass to his tight end. The Bulldogs were well short of the first-down marker and had to punt.

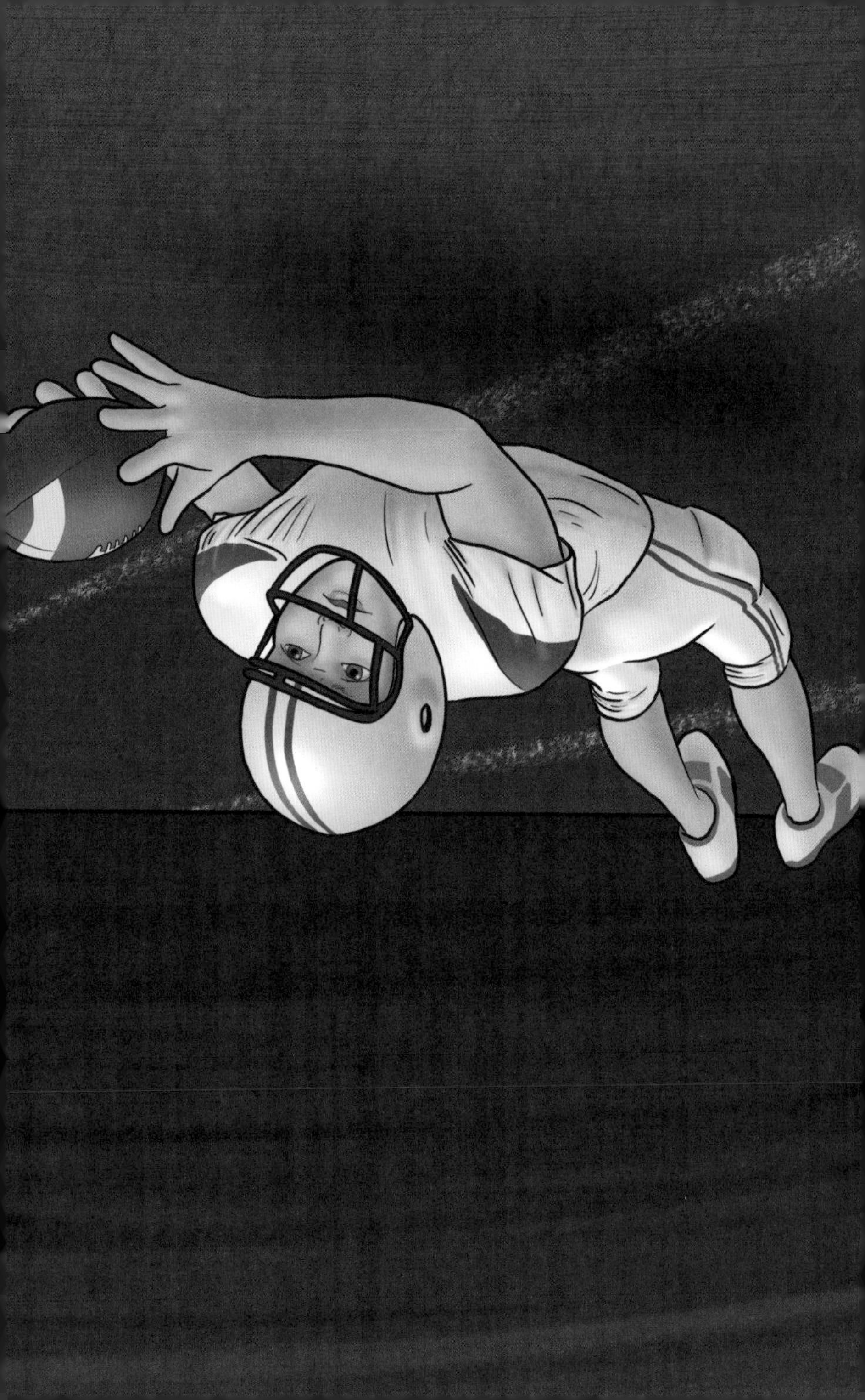

Chapter 31

The Big Game

Artesia's team was loaded, so they had good players at every position. Their punter could bomb the ball. He was getting scholarship offers from colleges throughout the state and region. He blasted a punt 55 yards down the field, and Brian fielded it cleanly. He darted right, slipping past the first Bulldog to make it down the field, and then accelerated toward midfield.

Brian spied a lane down the right sideline and cut across the field. When he passed midfield, Brian noticed something: He only had one player to beat—Artesia's punter. The punter wasn't a small guy, and he was trying to get a good angle on Brian. As he approached the punter at Artesia's 40-yard line, Brian had two choices: run out of bounds, or run his opponent over.

Brian picked the second option.

He lowered his shoulder and slammed into the Bulldogs punter. The punter bounced off of him like a cartoon character. Brian maintained his balance after the collision. Looking up, he saw nothing but green space.

"Go Brian, go!"

Even with 6,000 people at Wildcat Stadium, Brian could still hear his mother shouting words of support to him.

Brian scored, giving Lovington a 7-0 lead.

But Artesia rebounded on the very next series.

The Wildcats continued to gamble and Maupin completed a quick slant pass to his top receiver as the cornerback defending him blitzed. Once the receiver caught the ball, he only had to beat Lovington's other safety, and then he cruised down the field for a 48-yard touchdown.

The teams started piling up the points and Artesia led 24-21 with three minutes remaining.

The Bulldogs had assigned a cornerback and safety to double Brian on every snap of the game. That strategy worked because Brian had only four catches for 37 yards heading into the final drive of the game. But Brian wanted to make one more big play so they could finally help the Wildcats take down the Bulldogs.

Lovington's quarterback, Chris Paloma, had put together a nice game.

Entering the final huddle, Chris looked at Brian and said, "I need you."

Brian nodded.

Coach Faith called a play in which Chris threw a timed pass to a certain spot on the sideline. Either Brian was going to catch it or no one would. When the ball was snapped, Brian cut hard toward the middle of the field. The cornerback backpedaled and shadowed him, and the safety started to move toward him.

But after 12 yards, Brian sprinted toward the left sideline, creating a cushion between him and the two Bulldog defenders. Chris waited and waited, and then he chucked the ball toward the sideline.

As the ball approached the sideline, Brian jumped—his body parallel to the ground—and extended his arms as far as they would reach. The point of the ball slammed into his fingertips, and he started to squeeze his hands as hard, and as quickly, as he could. As he skidded to the ground, a cloud of dust formed around him.

There on the sideline, right in front of Coach Henderson, all eyes focused on Brian...who had the ball firmly in his grasp.

The sideline official signaled a catch, and Coach Henderson begrudgingly nodded, acknowledging Brian's gritty play.

Brian had gained 35 yards! They were just 22 yards from the end zone and the game-winning touchdown. Lovington then shifted its strategy. They wanted to run as much clock as possible so Artesia didn't have enough time to mount a comeback.

Just like college and pro teams, Lovington elected to run the ball so the clock kept running. An incomplete pass, on the other hand, would stop the game clock.

The Wildcats had to be careful. Play too conservatively and they might put the pressure on themselves with a fourth down. Get too aggressive, and they might score very quickly and give the powerful Bulldogs' offense one more chance to score.

The Wildcats, though, practiced this situation a lot. It's called the "two-minute drill"—a reference to the final two minutes of a game.

Chris was confident in their plan, but the thumb on his throwing hand was really hurting. He went over to the team doctor, who gently squeezed it.

"Ouch!" Chris screamed.

The thumb was already starting to swell, and Chris couldn't move it at all.

"I'm afraid your thumb is broken," Dr. Bob said. "It's not safe for you to play anymore."

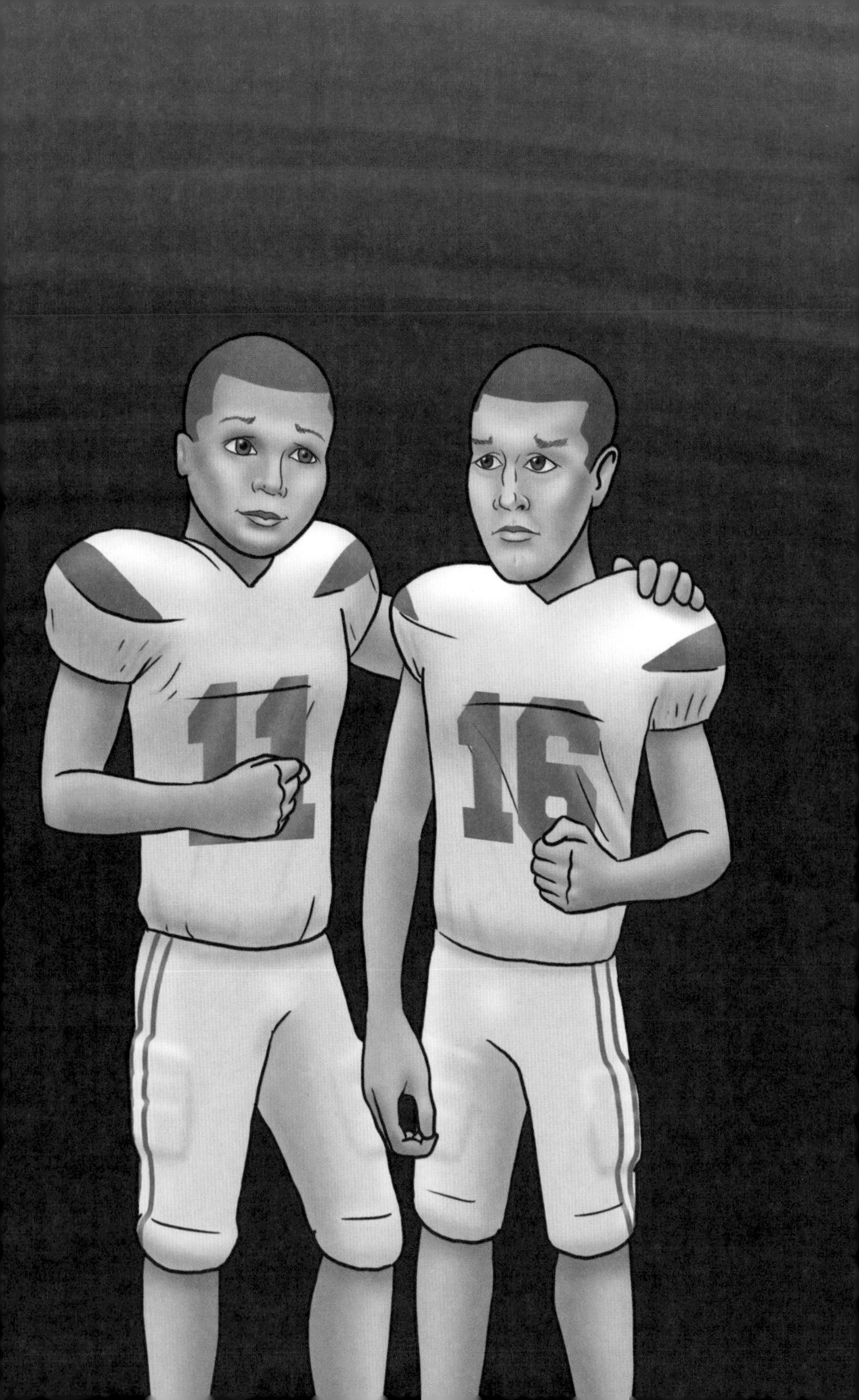
11
16

Chapter 32

Brandon Steps In

The gaze of everyone on the sideline shifted from Chris' thumb to Brian's best friend, Brandon. It took Brandon a moment to realize why they had all started staring at him. Brandon was the backup quarterback.

Being the backup quarterback may be the worst position in football. The backup is at practice and in every meeting, but he rarely gets to work with the offensive starters because the starting quarterback needs as many repetitions as possible. Then, if the starting quarterback gets hurt in a game, the backup is thrust into the lineup and expected to run the offense without missing a beat.

It's an impossible job—and Brandon had it worst of all. He was entering one of the most important games in Lovington sports' history. He didn't have any time to even attempt a few practice throws. He bolted toward the middle of the field, until he heard Coach Q screaming at him.

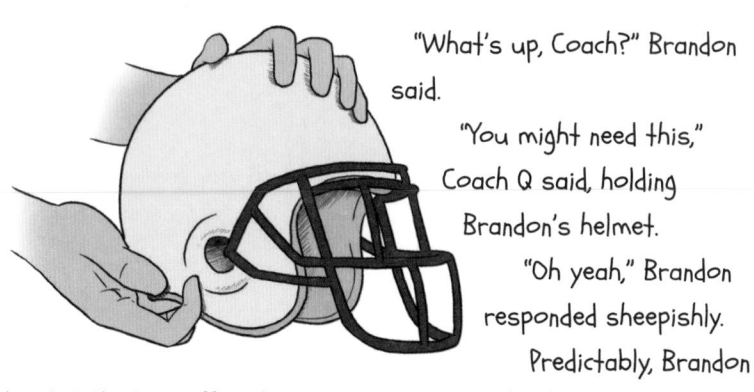

"What's up, Coach?" Brandon said.

"You might need this," Coach Q said, holding Brandon's helmet.

"Oh yeah," Brandon responded sheepishly.

Predictably, Brandon handed the ball off to his running backs on the first two plays. Coach Faith wanted Brandon to get into the flow of the game. On third down, Coach Faith called another running play, but Brandon didn't like the call, and he decided to call an audible.

A quarterback can call a different play than what a coach on the sideline wants if he notices something in the way the defense lines up. For instance, if the plan is to run the ball to the left, and the quarterback sees the defense shifting players that way, then the quarterback may call an audible. He can then bark out a command to instruct his teammates to run the ball to the right.

On the important third down play, Brandon noticed the linebackers were all very close to the line of scrimmage. They were expecting a run up the middle.

"Lobo 23!" Brandon shouted out.

His teammates were puzzled, but they played it cool.

Lobo 23 was a risky play that called for the quarterback to pitch the ball to Brian. Lovington's offensive players had to really think about the play because they had never practiced it!

When the ball was snapped to Brandon, the offensive line

blocked as if their running back was going to run right behind the center. Instead, though, Brandon turned and flipped the ball to his left, where Brian was alone.

Brian didn't have any blockers. The momentum of Artesia's defense was headed in the other direction. Brian only needed to beat the cornerback assigned to cover him. As the cornerback neared, Brian stiff-armed him and bolted up the left sideline. The safety tried to close in next, but Brian was just too fast.

Brian scored the touchdown from 17 yards out.

After the extra point, the Wildcats led 28–24. With no timeouts, Artesia didn't have enough time to pull off the miracle.

The Wildcats won!

When it was time to shake hands, Brian noticed that Jessie Cole, the running back who had called them losers after the championship game, was crying.

Should I stick it to him? Brian thought.

If anyone deserved to get razzed, Jessie certainly did. Brian decided that wasn't being a good sport. He just politely shook everyone's hands then rushed toward Brandon.

"We did it!" Brian said to Brandon.

But after one of the biggest wins in town history, the celebration was quiet as people learned that Chris wouldn't be able to play anymore. Could Lovington win a state title without Chris, their starting quarterback?

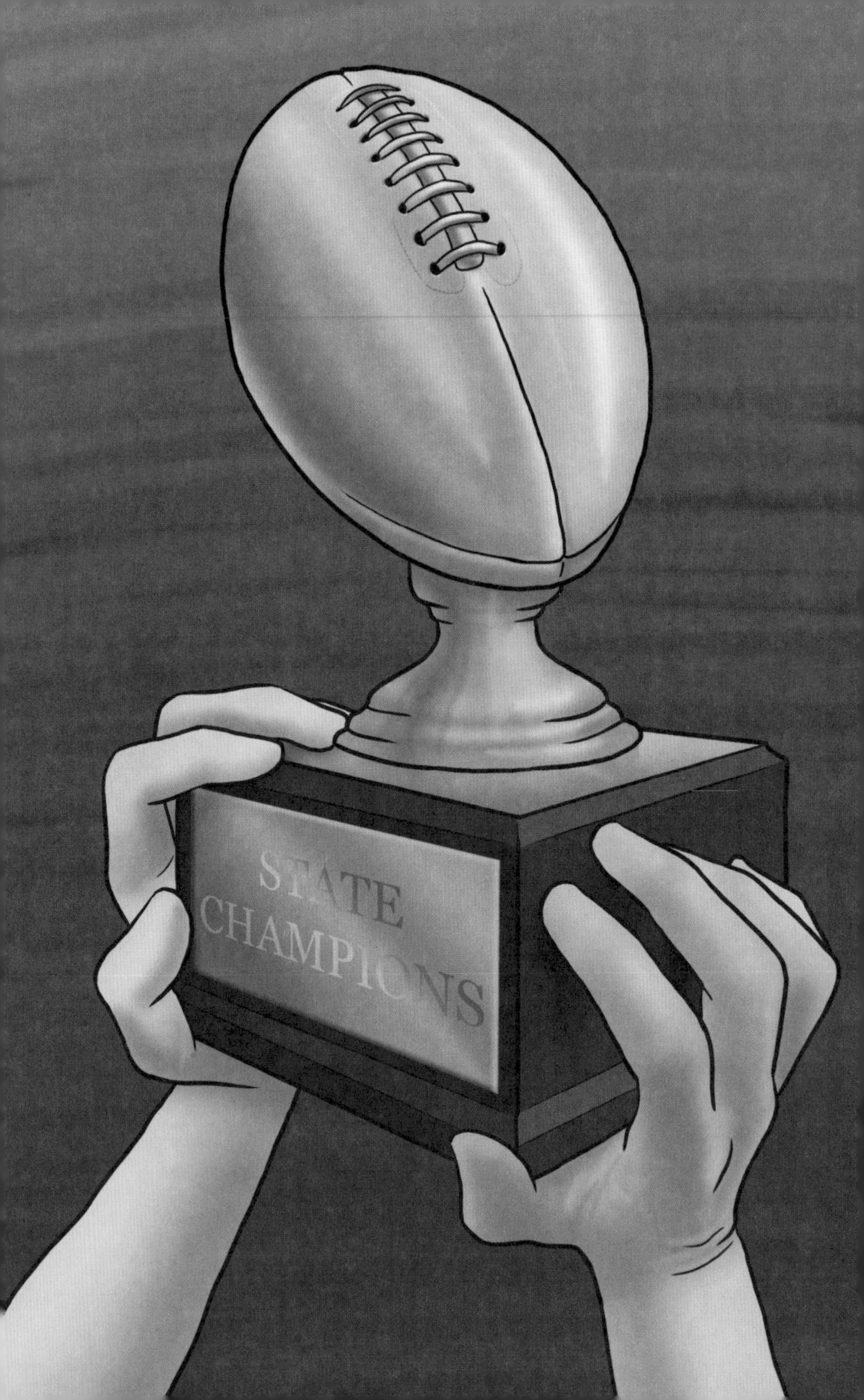
STATE
CHAMPIONS

Championship Moment

Brandon was a good athlete, but he hadn't really played football in a few years because he had focused on basketball. Brandon had paid attention to his football coaches in meetings though.

He and Brian spent extra time working on routes after Chris was sidelined with a broken thumb. It was just like the old days, when the best friends would draw up plays together and practice them!

Fortunately for Brandon, Lovington's final two regular-season opponents weren't very good. The Wildcats trounced Tucumcari and Kirtland Central by a combined score of 76-15.

Then, in the first round of the state tournament, Lovington destroyed Thoreau 84-0. The next game was also a breeze, a 33-7 win over Hot Springs. For a second consecutive season, Lovington had reached the championship game.

The Wildcats hadn't won a state title since the 1990 season, and Brian wanted to finish his career a champion.

The Wildcats had to play Silver City. The previous season, Silver City gave Lovington all they could handle. After missing games with a dislocated wrist, Brian's first game back was against Silver City, and Lovington barely won the game 10-7.

After the first quarter in the championship game, the Wildcats had built a 14-7 lead. The Fighting Colts were mounting a strong drive just before halftime. Their quarterback dropped back and lofted a pass toward a receiver who was wide open. But Brian sprinted toward the ball, then turned and jumped as high as he could into the air. He reached back with only his right arm and pulled the ball in.

Brian had intercepted the pass.

The mouths of Silver City's coaches and players dropped.

The Fighting Colts didn't have much fight in them after Brian's big play. Brandon and Brian were playing pitch and catch, like they had as kids. They were completely locked in. Brandon knew where Brian wanted the ball. Brian knew where Brandon wanted him to be.

Midway through third quarter, Brandon heaved a pass as far as he could throw it. Brian used his speed to run under it for a 42-yard touchdown. The Wildcats then controlled the remainder of the game and closed out the championship 24–7.

The Wildcats were champions!

"We did it!" Brian's mother shouted over and over.

She and Troy raced toward the field, where they wrapped Brian and Casey in big bear hugs.

"I'm so proud of you boys," she said. "You worked so hard for this."

She smothered Brian and Casey in kisses, but neither of them minded.

Epilogue

The Wildcats went 14–0 to win the 3A state football championship. Brian played every single down on offense, defense, and special teams. He had learned the secrets to success on the football field: a strong work ethic, integrity, and valuing the team above the individual.

As a receiver, Brian had 61 catches for 1,348 yards and 15 touchdowns. As a returner, he had six touchdowns. As a running back, he scored twice, and he returned one interception for a touchdown as well.

His numbers could have been much grander, but he wanted his teammates to get a chance to score touchdowns and make plays too.

Brian also had a memorable senior season in basketball. Even though he barely played in eighth grade, he was named to the prestigious All-State team after leading the Wildcats in points (25) and rebounds (15) per game.

Despite his high school success, Brian received a scholarship offer from one Division I school—the University of New Mexico. After a coaching change before his junior year, Brian flourished in the Lobos defense and also contributed as a returner and receiver. As a senior, Brian was a first-team All-American, and he even finished 12th in balloting for the Heisman Trophy.

The Dallas Cowboys didn't draft Brian. But the Chicago Bears made him the ninth overall pick of the 2000 NFL Draft, and Brian didn't disappoint. He became the face of the historic franchise, earning eight Pro Bowl selections and being named the 2005 Associated Press NFL Defensive Player of the Year. The Bears reached Super Bowl XLI, in February 2007, but they were defeated 29–17 by the Indianapolis Colts.

Brian retired after the 2012 NFL season, and he's eligible for enshrinement in the Pro Football Hall of Fame in 2018.

After serving as an analyst for Fox Sports 1 during the 2013 NFL season, Brian stepped away from that role and focused on spending time with his daughters, Pamela and Riley, and his son, Kennedy.

SEAN JENSEN was born in South Korea. He was adopted and grew up in California, Massachusetts, and Virginia, mostly on or near military bases. Given his unique background, he's always been drawn to storytelling—a skill he developed at Northwestern University and crafted as a sportswriter for the last 16 years, almost exclusively covering the NFL During his career, he's fostered strong relationships with athletes in multiple sports, and penned award-winning features on Derrick Rose and Adrian Peterson, among others.

MY THOUGHTS

MY THOUGHTS

MY THOUGHTS

MY THOUGHTS